# A MANAGER'S GUIDE TO
# SELF-DEVELOPMENT

# A MANAGER'S GUIDE TO
# SELF-DEVELOPMENT

Mike Pedler
John Burgoyne
Tom Boydell

McGRAW-HILL Book Company (UK) Limited

London · New York · St Louis · San Francisco · Auckland · Beirut · Bogotá
Düsseldorf · Johannesburg · Lisbon · Lucerne · Madrid · Mexico · Montreal
New Delhi · Panama · Paris · San Juan · São Paulo · Singapore · Sydney
Tokyo · Toronto

Published by
McGraw-Hill Book Company (UK) Limited
Maidenhead · Berkshire · England

**Library of Congress Cataloging in Publication Data**
Pedler, Mike
    A manager's guide to self-development
    1. Management
    I. Title II. Burgoyne, John III. Boydell, Tom
    658.4   HD31   77-30174
    ISBN 0-07-084500-X

1234 W.C. & S. 7987

Printed and bound in Great Britain

# Contents

# 1. The philosophy of the book

This book, which is an aid to management self-development rather than a repository of wisdom, is based on a simple fundamental premise:

> that any effective system for management development must increase the manager's capacity and willingness to take control over and responsibility for events, and particularly for himself and his own learning.

This is not a new concept, and the approach we derive from it is not new either. However, it is one that is far from recognized in current society and by management in particular.

Most of us, if asked to think about how we have learned, think of our experiences in situations where attempts have been made to *teach* us.[1] If, on the other hand, we are asked about *problems we have solved* we think about difficult situations we have faced and managed to overcome. But in solving problems we do not just deal with an immediate difficulty, we also discover a solution that we may be able to use again in some form, and we may also become better at solving problems generally. Problem solving *is* to a large extent *learning*.

The fact that confronting real problems, rather than being taught, is the major source of significant learning or development is well recognized, at least implicitly, in the managerial world. When it comes to a 'crunch' decision, like selecting a new senior manager, what really counts is whether the candidate has coped successfully with a number of situations which were seen by those involved as difficult. Information on what he* has *been taught*, through involvement in formal management development programmes, is often not seen as important enough to take into account in senior management promotion decisions. When it is taken into account there is no evidence that it is anything more than a minor factor.[2]

The implication for the manager who is ambitious in career terms is clear: *get a slice of the action, deal with it in a way that is clearly successful*, and *be seen to have done it* (the visibility factor).

* We use "male" pronouns throughout this book for the sake of brevity, rather than to reinforce the "male" image of management, which is the reverse of our preferences.

We believe that the reason why formal management development has not really 'made it' as a significant force is that it has, unintentionally, *deskilled* managers. This needs explaining. It is now some years since Marshal McLuhan gave us the simple but powerful thought that *the medium is the message*.[3] He pointed out that the major impact of books and television has been much less to do with the content or messages, in the pages or programmes, and much more to do with the form of the medium and its implications at the psychological and social level. The printed word made ideas and knowledge mass-producible, so that they ceased to be the exclusive province of a well-educated elite who could use them to control others. No wonder they burnt books! Television makes the dissemination of ideas and knowledge instant, and creates the possibility of identical messages being pumped into the minds of large numbers of people who have become conditioned to the television as a source of mind-filling material which is in turn attuned to their needs for entertainment, information, and so on by a system which seeks to maximize ratings.

The *messages* from formal management development may be concerned with discounted cash flow, leadership skills, critical path planning, or corporate strategy, but what is the *medium* doing? The messages coming from the medium are, we suggest:

> There is an expert for every type of management problem; don't try to solve them on your own—call in the experts.

> You don't know how to learn? Don't worry, you don't need to. We are here to manage it for you. If you need a 'retread' don't try to do it yourself, come back to us.

These messages, we believe, deskill managers. This is why we are attempting to provide in this book a vehicle for *self*-development based on the premise that effective management development must increase a manager's capacity and willingness to take control over, and responsibility for, events.

## What is self-development?

For the sake of brevity, here is a simple answer to what is really a complex issue. We define self-development as personal development, with the manager taking primary responsibility for his own learning and for choosing the means to achieve this. Other commonly held views on the meaning and purposes of self-development are:

> —career development and advancement;
> —improving performance in an existing job;
> —developing certain specific qualities or skills;
> —achieving total potential—self-actualization.

This book is designed to help with all of these, particularly the last three. Self-development may well lead to advancement; our primary concern is with the development of managers at all levels.

The book is an invitation to work on your own personal development, and to accept our suggestions on strategy and tactics, working with the resources we have provided.

REFERENCES

1. Kolb, D. A., I. M. Rubin and J. M. McIntyre, *Organisational Psychology: An Experimental Approach*, Prentice-Hall Inc., 1971, p. 27.
2. Glickman, A. S., C. P. Hahn, E. A. Fleishman and B. Baxter, *Top Management Succession*, MacMillan, New York, 1968.
3. McLuhan, M., *Understanding Media: The Extensions of Man*, Sphere, 1964.

# 2. How the book works

If you are interested in having a go at this self-development programme you will need first to take some time thinking about where you are now and where you want to be in terms of work and career activities, in thinking about the skills you have and those you need to develop, and in working out learning goals and planning a personal learning programme.

You are likely to have only limited, and unpredictable time periods to carry out the project. This book is designed, therefore, so that you can work on some of the exercises a bit at a time, using odd half hours on train journeys, between meetings—in the bath, or in bed if you are keen enough. Some of the activities need to be tackled at work, such as observing how meetings work and trying out different forms of personal intervention. Others you can work through in informal contact with colleagues, over lunch for instance, to test their perceptions against your own.

Finally, you face an apparent paradox. If you work on a self-development project in which *you* take responsibility for deciding what you need to learn and how to learn it, on what basis are you to accept help from other sources including, obviously, the authors of this book? There is no paradox as long as you accept that the book offers suggestions rather than instructions. It is for you to decide at each stage whether what we suggest is right for you, and whether there is a better way that you can think of for yourself. We suggest (but do not instruct) that you spend time, if you work through parts of this book, considering whether you can improve on our suggestions *for yourself*. Keep in mind our explanation that the book is a series of suggestions and that you will only learn if you decide for yourself whether to follow the suggestions or not. Because it would be cumbersome to begin every sentence 'we suggest that you consider . . .' or 'one way to look at this is to consider that . . .', much of the rest of the book will give straightforward descriptions of things to do, and make blunt assertions about management, which may tend to sound like instructions, commands, orders, or statements of ultimate truth. This is for clarity and brevity. Remember, it is for *you to decide* whether to believe our interpretations of reality or accept our suggestions.

The book is in two parts. The first is designed to help you set learning goals for yourself and to help you plan to achieve these goals. The second is designed to help you carry out that plan.

We suggest that you work through the first part sequentially, using the 'life planning' option incorporated in it, if appropriate. When you reach the end of Part 1 you should have a list of areas in which you recognize the need to develop yourself.

Part 2 consists of a set of resources, in the form of exercises and other suggested activities which you can use to achieve some of your learning goals. Part 1 ends with some general suggestions on how to use the activities, and a guide, in the form of the 'Learning Goal Matrix', which shows which activities might help you achieve which learning goals.

Finally, there is an Appendix, 'A Note for Management Trainers', which sets out some guidelines for management teachers or trainers who may be using these activities as part of their courses and programmes.

# Part 1
## Setting and meeting goals for management self-development

# 3. A life planning activity

Since this book is intended as an aid to personal development for management it is primarily oriented to helping those who have already satisfied themselves that management is for them, and are concerned about what they want to achieve within a managerial career, and how to achieve it.

However, personal situations are rarely that neat, and it is necessary to raise initially the questions of what we want to do with our lives, and how we are to decide.

> First, you may be interested in personal development as a way of finding out whether you could be a manager, particularly a good manager, and whether you *want* to be.

> Second, you may be firmly committed to a managerial career, but be unclear *why*. It might help you to clarify why you are committed to being a manager and what kind of personal needs it satisfies, so that you can see more clearly what you want to do within your managerial career.

Before we ask you to consider whether you should spend time working on the issues of your total life goals and life plan, try this—the first 'activity' in the book:

> Answer the following questions:

> Assuming one day's work equals about eight hours direct work activity, how many days have you put into systematically locating and finding out about alternatives, clarifying personal priorities and criteria, and assessing alternatives in connection with three decisions:

>> choosing the last car you bought?
>> selecting the house you now live in?
>> planning your life?

> Now rank the same three decisions in order of importance.

> Does this give you any feelings about whether you should spend some time on life planning?

If you feel that you would like to give some attention to life planning, proceed with the following activity, which has been widely used, tried, and tested for personal and organization development purposes.

The activity is in the form of a series of questions and small tasks designed to give you insight into your needs, ambitions, skills, potential, and opportunities, and encourage you to think systematically about the future and what you may wish to do about it.

How much you get out of the activity depends on how much you put in. The more effort you put into working through the questions as they apply to you the more insights you will get.

The learning and payoff from the activity can be increased if you discuss your answers with someone else whom you trust and whose opinions you value. In fact, an ideal way to work through the activity is with one or two other persons, with whom you share and discuss each other's answers to each question.

To do the activity properly takes time. A group is likely to need a day or two to work through it. If you are working alone, you could tackle it a little at a time, setting yourself an objective to complete one question each day.

## A life planning activity[1]

1. Below you will find a time line. The far left side represents the day of your birth; the far right side the day of your death. Draw a line like it on a piece of paper and place a mark on it which represents where you see yourself being today. Place today's date under your mark.

_____

What does the position of your mark tell you about how to see your future and your past? Write some notes and discuss them with someone.

2. Next, try to focus on your past. Consider the part of the line which extends from your birth to where you are today. Blow it up and draw a line to represent your life. Be as creative as you can in illustrating your life line, putting in the peaks, troughs, and plateaux.

Example:

*Figure 3.1*

As you look at your life line, what are the moments which stand out as being of most importance to you? What are some things you would like to avoid repeating in the future? What are some of the things you would like to re-create again in the future? Discuss your life line with someone, and jot down any insights that come as a result.

**3.** List up to ten adjectives which describe you most accurately with regard to:

(a)  Your CAREER

(b)  Your PERSONAL RELATIONSHIPS

(c)  MATERIAL WEALTH and POSSESSIONS

(d)  Your OWN PERSONAL DEVELOPMENT AND LEARNING

(e) From the above four lists, select the ten adjectives which are most important in describing you. Rank them in order (i)–(x).

(i)

(ii)

(iii)

(iv)

(v)

(vi)

(vii)

(viii)

(ix)

(x)

Now go back through all your five lists of adjectives making each one either

+ for POSITIVE
− for NEGATIVE
0 for NEUTRAL

Discuss your lists with your partner(s) until you have a rounded picture of yourself and how you feel about this picture.

**4.** So far you have been concentrating on the past and what it has been like for you. Now you are going to look ahead and imagine what it will be like. Unlike the past, the future is unknown so that you need to be as imaginative and creative as you can be in describing *how you would like it to be.*
Now write about one of the following:

(a) Think about some day in the distant future. The day is perfect in the sense that it includes all those things in it that you would like to have for yourself. Describe this day in some detail.

(b) Write your own obituary as it might appear in *The Times.*

When you have done this, read it and discuss it with your partner(s). What sort of goals do you have for your life? You might want to jot down some comments as a result of your discussion.

**5.** Now you are going to look at your life goals in a more systematic way. The idea here is to consider *all* the goals that are important to you in *all* areas of your life. Be honest with yourself, it's your life you're planning.
Fill in your own goals below. Five sections are listed but feel free to add to them if necessary. Be as specific as you are able. Think in terms of three to five years ahead.

(a) CAREER GOALS

Goals for your future job or career.

(i)

(ii)

(iii)

### (b) PERSONAL RELATIONSHIP GOALS

Goals for your relationships with colleagues, friends, parents, children, people in general.

(i)

(ii)

(iii)

### (c) MATERIAL GOALS

Goals for your standard of living, what possessions do you want?

(i)

(ii)

(iii)

### (d) PERSONAL DEVELOPMENT GOALS

Goals for your own learning and development. What would you like to know? to be able to do? to become?

(i)

(ii)

(iii)

### (e) OTHER IMPORTANT LIFE GOALS

Other goals not in the categories (a)–(d), e.g., spiritual, leisure, status.

(i)

(ii)

(iii)

(f) Now go back over all your goals and rate the IMPORTANCE of each as either:

H—Compared to my other goals this is very important.
M—This goal is moderately important.
L—A lot of other goals are more important than this one.

(g) Now go back over all your goals again and rate the PROBABILITY of ATTAINMENT of each as either:

(i) Compared with other goals I can easily reach this one.
(ii) Moderately difficult to reach and maintain this one.
(iii) Very difficult to reach and maintain.

## (h) GOAL PRIORITY

Select from all your goals above, the ones that seem most important at this time. Do not choose more than five. Rank them in order of importance.

(i)

(ii)

(iii)

(iv)

(v)

Now discuss this section with your partner(s). Where do these goals come from? Did you choose them or did your parents or society put them forward? Are they consistent with one another?

## 6. STRATEGIC GOAL PLANNING

(a) Think of a date one year from now. Draw up a short list of intermediate goals you would like to have accomplished one year from today. (Not more than five.)

(i)

(ii)

(iii)

(iv)

(v)

Discuss this short list with your partner(s). This is where his/her or their help might be most vital. Make sure the following questions are answered to everyone's satisfaction:

—How realistic are these strategic goals?
—What are your chances of success?

—Are they congruent with your life goals?
—Are they in conflict with each other?
—How will you feel when you attain these goals—what will it feel like?
—How will you feel if you do not attain these goals—what will happen?

(b) You might need to define your strategic goals more clearly to continue here. This stage helps you plan the achievement of these goals. For each goal you must examine four issues:

(i) Personal shortcomings to be overcome.
(ii) Obstacles in the world to overcome.
(iii) Actions I can take to achieve this goal.
(iv) Help I need from others.

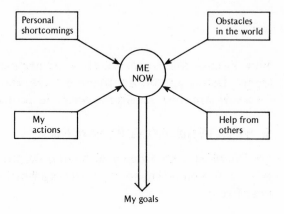

Figure 3.2

This section is difficult but ultimately very rewarding. It might help to work on it jointly with a partner. You can try questioning each other and even filling in the answers for each other after discussion. Being able to express the goals and obstacles helps clarify them.

(c)  Complete a sheet like this for *each* strategic goal that you want to achieve by one year from today.

*What personal shortcomings will keep me from achieving* ...........................?

  (i)

 (ii)

(iii)

 (iv)


*What can I do to eliminate or lessen the effects of these obstacles or shortcomings?*

*Obstacle/shortcoming*       *What I can do about it*


*What specific things can I do to move me towards this goal?*

  (i)

 (ii)

(iii)

 (iv)

Underline the one you are going to emphasize most.

*Who can help me with this goal and what will I ask of them?*

*Who can help?*                 *With what?*

### 7. NOW WHAT?

There is no end to the detailed action steps and plans you can make to help you achieve strategic goals. The overall purpose of the activity has been to help you establish where you are and where you want to go in your life and career.

If you want to take the goal and target setting further, here are some suggestions:*

(a) Establish a programme schedule with specific steps and deadlines for each strategic goal with assessment points at every deadline. To do this you will need to describe the goal in *measurable* terms. You can do it in the form of a graph:

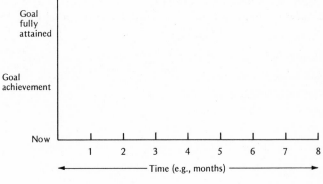

*Figure 3.3*

(b) Other people are one of your major resources for goal achievement. Establish a written contract with another person to help you achieve a given strategic goal.

Obviously you can do (a) and (b) together.

### REFERENCES

1. There are many versions of this activity. For another example see D. A. Kolb *et al.*, *Organisational Psychology: An Experiential Approach*, Prentice-Hall Inc., 1971, pp. 273–293.

* Activity 27, 'Action Planning', is an alternative format for doing this further planning.

# 4. Some ideas about management and the qualities of successful managers

One way in which we might have designed a book on management self-development would have been to present you with a number of exercises, more or less at random. We have been more methodical and have based the programme on our ideas of just what does contribute to managerial success.

Before discovering what our ideas are, you might like to stop right now and jot down your own views so that you can compare them with ours. Don't read ours yet but write down . . .

   —what you think are the main features of a manager's job, and what *is* management;

   —what you think are the main qualities required to be a successful manager.

Our own views are based on a combination of our own experience, of reading widely about management and the nature of management work, and above all on a research project carried out by one of us.

The project identified a number of qualities which were found to be possessed by successful managers and not possessed by less successful managers. As a double check, three different sets of 'successful' managers were used:

   —those who had risen to senior posts;

   —up-and-coming managers who were significantly younger than average for their level of seniority (whiz-kids);

   —managers of any age and level who were recognized as doing their job with above average effectiveness.

Table 4.1 shows some of the success patterns related to these criteria. Before reading on past the table, ask yourself two seemingly simple questions. (We suggest that you write down the answers. We find that the extra effort

| SUCCESS/EFFECTIVENESS DIMENSIONS | | | SUCCESS PATTERNS |
|---|---|---|---|
| *Holding senior responsibility* | *Career progress* | *Immediate task effectiveness* | |
| More successful (i.e., relatively senior level) | More successful (i.e., relatively swift promotion to this level) | More successful | Young senior manager, maintaining interest and performance |
| | | Less successful | Young senior manager, beginning to 'sit back' |
| | Less successful (i.e., relatively slow promotion to this level) | More successful | Older senior manager having progressed slowly up the career ladder, strongly committed to effective work |
| | | Less successful | Older senior manager, having progressed slowly up the career ladder, beginning to slacken off |
| Less successful (i.e., relatively junior level) | More successful (i.e., relatively swift promotion to this level) | More successful | Promising younger manager performing effectively in a relatively responsible job for his age |
| | | Less successful | Younger manager not performing too well in a relatively senior job. Possibly there by virtue of patronage, inertia from earlier success, or insensitive fast track system |
| | Less successful (i.e., relatively slow promotion to this level) | More successful | Older manager performing an essential, if relatively junior job, with high degree of effectiveness |
| | | Less successful | Older manager whose performance has not kept up with the demands of a relatively junior job |

*Table 4.1*

involved in committing thoughts to paper pays off well in terms of what people can get from an exercise of this nature.)

Here are the questions:

    —Where do I stand now in terms of Table 4.1?
    —How do I feel about this? (Jot down quickly a number of words/ phrases which sum up these feelings; don't think too deeply about them as you are writing them, put them down—as they come into your head.)

The research identified 10 attributes which were found to be possessed by the successful managers, and since then we have added another. These 11 qualities, or attributes, form the basis of the programme of self-development provided in this book:

1. Command of basic facts
✓ 2. Relevant professional knowledge
3. Continuing sensitivity to events
4. Analytical, problem-solving, decision/judgement-making skills
✓ 5. Social skills and abilities
✓ 6. Emotional resilience
7. Proactivity—inclination to respond purposefully to events
8. Creativity
9. Mental agility
10. Balanced learning habits and skills
11. Self-knowledge

These qualities fall into three groups, which constitute three different levels.

Numbers 1 and 2 form the foundation level: they represent two kinds of basic knowledge and information that a manager may need to use in making decisions and taking action.

Numbers 3 to 7 are specific skills and attributes that directly affect behaviour and performance. Number 3 is the skill or quality that allows managers to acquire the basic knowledge and information involved in 1 and 2.

Numbers 8 to 11 are those qualities which allow the manager to develop and deploy his skills and resources in categories 3, 4, and 5. They may be called 'meta-qualities' because they allow the manager to develop the situation-specific skills needed in particular circumstances. See Fig. 4.1.

Many of the attributes are interconnected—that is, possession of one contributes to possession of another.

Below is a short explanation of each of these 11 attributes, providing our basic model for self-development.

### Basic knowledge and information

#### 1. Command of basic facts

Successful managers know what's what in their organization. They have a command of such basic facts as goals and plans (long- and short-term), product knowledge, who's who in the organization, the roles and relationships between various departments, their own job and what's expected of them. If they don't store all this information, they know where to get it when they need it.

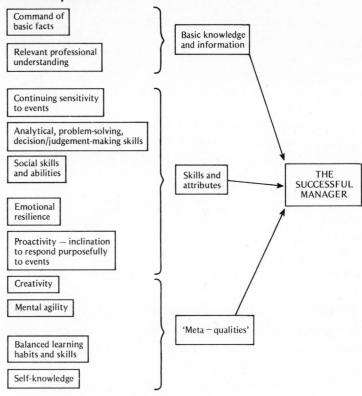

*Figure 4.1. Eleven qualities of a successful manager*

### 2. Relevant professional knowledge

This category includes 'technical' knowledge, e.g., production technology, marketing techniques, engineering knowledge, relevant legislation, sources of finance, and knowledge of basic background management principles and theories, e.g., planning, organizing, and controlling.

## Skills

### 3. Continuing sensitivity to events

Managers vary in the degree to which they can sense what is happening in a particular situation. The successful manager is relatively sensitive to events and can tune in to what's going on around him. He is perceptive and open to information—'hard' information, such as figures and facts, and 'soft' information, such as the feelings of other people. The manager with this sensitivity is able to respond in an appropriate way to situations as they arise.

### 4. Analytical, problem-solving, and decision/judgement-making skills

The job of the manager is very much concerned with making decisions. Sometimes these can be made using logical, optimizing techniques. Other decisions call for the ability to weigh pros and cons in what is basically a very uncertain or ambiguous situation, calling for a high level of judgement or even intuition. The manager must therefore develop judgement-making skills, including the ability to cope with ambiguity and uncertainty, striking a balance between the necessity at times to be guided by his subjective feelings without throwing objective logic completely out of the window.

### 5. Social skills and abilities

One definition of management often cited is 'getting things done through other people'. This definition may be inadequate, but it does point to one of  the key features of the manager's job—it requires interpersonal skills. The successful manager develops a range of abilities which are essential in such activities: communicating, delegating, negotiating, resolving conflict, persuading, selling, using and responding to authority and power.

## Personal qualities

### 6. Emotional resilience

The manager's job involves a degree of emotional stress and strain, which arises as a natural consequence of working in situations involving authority, leadership, power, interpersonal conflict, meeting targets and deadlines, all within a framework of a degree of uncertainty and ambiguity.

The successful manager needs to be sufficiently resilient to cope with this. 'Resilient' means that he feels the stress (he doesn't become thick-skinned and insensitive) but is able to cope with it by maintaining self-control and by 'giving' to some extent, but not so much that he becomes permanently deformed.

### 7. Proactivity—inclination to respond purposefully to events

Effective managers have some purpose or goal to achieve, rather than merely responding to demand. They cannot plan everything carefully in advance, and at times they must respond to the needs of the instant situation, but when making such a response the effective manager manages to consider the longer term. He relates immediate responses to overall and longer-term aims and goals, whereas the less successful manager responds in a relatively unthinking or uncritical way to the immediate pressure. This category of ability also includes such qualities as seeing a job through, being dedicated and committed, having a sense of mission, and taking responsibility for things that happen rather than passing the buck to someone else.

## 8. Creativity

By 'creativity' we mean the ability to come up with unique new responses to situations, and to have the breadth of insight to recognize and take up useful new approaches. It involves not only having new ideas oneself, but also the ability to recognize a good idea when it is presented from another source.

## 9. Mental agility

Although related to general intelligence level, the concept of 'mental agility' includes the ability to grasp problems quickly, to think of several things at once, to switch rapidly from one problem or situation to another, to see quickly the whole situation (rather than ponderously plough through all its components), and to 'think on one's feet'. Given the hectic nature of managerial work these are particularly necessary qualities for success.

## 10. Balanced learning habits and skills

Data collected by observing and interviewing managers show that a significant proportion of the degree of their success can be explained by the presence or absence of habits and skills related to learning.

—Successful managers are more independent as learners; they take responsibility for the 'rightness' of what is learned, rather than depending, passively and uncritically, on an authority figure (a teacher or an expert) to define 'truths'.

—Successful managers are capable of abstract thinking, as well as concrete, practical thought. They are able to relate concrete ideas to abstract ones (and vice versa) relatively quickly. This ability—which is sometimes known as a 'helicopter mind'—enables the manager to generate his own theories from practice, and to develop his own practical ideas from theory.

—The ability to use a range of different learning processes is necessary for managerial success. Three such processes are:

   (a)  input—receiving expository teaching, either formal (e.g., on a course) or informal (e.g., coaching by a colleague);

   (b)  discovery—generating personal meaning from one's own experiences;

   (c)  reflection—a process of analysing and reorganizing pre-existing experiences and ideas.

—Successful managers are more likely to have a relatively wide view of the nature of the skills of management. For example, they are more likely to recognize the range of managerial attributes as presented in this model, than to believe that management is a unitary activity, involving, for example, dealing with subordinates (i.e., needing only a certain set of social skills) or simply involving basic decision making.

## 11. Self-knowledge

Whatever the manager does is in some way affected by his own view of his job and his role, by his goals, his values, his feelings, his strengths and weaknesses, and a host of other personal or 'self' factors. If, then, he is to retain a relatively high degree of self-control over his actions, he must be aware of these self-attributes and of the part they are playing in determining his behaviour. The successful manager must therefore develop skills of introspection.

## Summary: So what?

One of the fundamental beliefs underlying this book is that everything written here is our opinion. It is essential, if the book is to succeed as an aid to your self-development, that you decide the extent to which you share our opinions, and what they mean, personally, to you.

Therefore, having read this chapter, write down your reactions to it. How do you feel already about what we have written? Interested? Bored? Sceptical? Enthusiastic? In agreement? In disagreement? Do our views match yours? What are your other reactions?

One of the activities (Activity 6) involves the keeping of a personal journal, the idea being to keep note of your on-going experiences, to identify your feelings about these experiences, and so learn from them. You may consider that reading these first chapters is an experience right for inclusion in the journal; if so, we suggest you work through Activity 6 now, before proceeding further.

## REFERENCES

1. Burgoyne, J. G. and R. Stuart, 'The nature, use and acquisition of managerial skills and other attributes', *Personnel Review*, 5, 4, 1976, pp. 19–29.

# 5. Assessing yourself and setting some goals for self-development

In chapter 4 we described our model of the qualities of effective managers. As we explained, we are using this model as the basis around which to build the activities which form the second part of this book.

One way of approaching the activities is to work through them in the order in which they appear. A better alternative is to determine your own priority areas and concentrate first on these. This chapter describes ways in which you might do this, involving three stages:

    —diagnosis
    —goal setting
    —planning for on-going evaluation

Different people will prefer different methods—it is up to each person to choose which he/she prefers. You might like to try out more than one method; if so, it will be interesting to compare the results to see to what extent they differ or concur.

## Method one: simple introspection

### Step 1. Diagnosis

The 11 qualities of effective managers are listed in column 1 of Table 5.1.

Consider yourself in terms of each quality in turn. How well equipped are you in each case? How much of the quality do you possess and to what extent would you like to develop it further? Think carefully about this. To help with this process, Table 5.1 presents you with some questions which you can ask yourself in connection with each of the 11 areas.

When you have interviewed yourself in this way, indicate your views by ticking or encircling the figures 1, 2, 3, or 4 which you will see in column 2 of Table 5.2.*

* Table 5.2 is also used in our second method of self-diagnosis: 'Conversation with a partner'. If you are trying both methods for comparison, make a copy of Table 5.2 before writing on it.

| Quality | Indicative questions |
|---|---|
| 1. Command of basic facts | —How much do you know about what's going on in your organization?<br>—What are your sources of information?<br>—How extensive are your contacts?<br>—How many people do you know in your organization?<br>—What do you know about the way other people feel about your organization? 'Other people' should include those superior to you, at your own level, more junior to yourself, owners, management, and workforce; customers, consumers, and clients.<br>—Can you think of some recent examples of occasions when you needed to know more basic facts?<br>—How much do you know about your organization's policies?<br>—How much do you know about your organization's medium- and long-term plans?<br>—What do you do to keep informed about all these things? |
| 2. Relevant professional knowledge | —What do you do to keep up-to-date with new techniques and with the latest thinking in your area?<br>—How much time do you spend reading specialist journals?<br>—How do you get guidance on technical or specialist aspects of your job?<br>—How well-informed are you about possible legislative, governmental, and international changes and the effect these might have on your organization? |
| 3. Continuing sensitivity to events | —What do you do to make sure that you are tuned in to what's happening in a given situation?<br>—How sensitive are you to the way other people are feeling, or to the way in which they are likely to react? What steps do you take to develop this sensitivity?<br>—How perceptive are you?<br>—How do you make sure that your assumptions about what's going on are correct?<br>—What types of situation do you find hardest to weigh up? |

Table 5.1. Some indicative questions to help you to give yourself a self-rating on the 11 qualities of an effective manager

| Quality | Indicative questions |
|---|---|
| 4. Problem-solving, analytical, and decision/judgement-making skills | —What do you find most difficult about making decisions?<br>—How do you feel about having to make judgements in situations in which ideally you would have more information?<br>—What range of decision-making techniques do you have available to help you when appropriate?<br>—Can you think of some recent examples of good and bad decisions you made?<br>—In general, how confident are you in your decision-making abilities? |
| 5. Social skills and abilities | —How much difficulty do you have with other people? What types of such difficulty do you have?<br>—What do you do in situations involving interpersonal conflict?<br>—Can you think of some recent examples of situations in which you needed to use social skills? What happened?<br>—How much do you know about what other people think and feel about you?<br>—How do you respond to anger, hostility, suspicion?<br>—How do you try to ensure that other people understand you when you communicate with them? How do you ensure that you understand others? |
| 6. Emotional resilience | —How do you cope with feelings of stress, tension, anxiety, fatigue?<br>—With whom do you discuss your worries and anxieties?<br>—Think of the most tense, stressful situations that you have been in recently. How did you behave?<br>—What do you do when you become emotional?<br>—How do you behave in situations of great ambiguity? (i.e., when you don't know what's going to happen next, when everything seems very uncertain). Can you give some examples?<br>—What do you do to make sure that you neither become thick-skinned nor over-affected by emotions? |

*Table 5.1. continued*

| Quality | Indicative questions |
| --- | --- |
| 7. Proactivity—inclination to respond purpose-fully to events | —What steps do you take to ensure that you're in control of your own behaviour, rather than allowing yourself to be controlled or manipulated by others or by situational pressures?<br>—In which situations do you tend to be independent and proactive as compared with situations in which you tend to be dependent and reactive?<br>—How good are you at taking the initiative?<br>—To what extent are you thrusting, active, self-starting, rather than sleeping, passive, following? |
| 8. Creativity | —How easy do you find it to come up with new ideas?<br>—How do you feel when all the well-tried solutions to a problem have failed?<br>—What do you do to try to see new ways of doing things?<br>—How often do you try out new methods, approaches, and solutions to problems?<br>—What are the most creative things you have done in the past 12 months?<br>—How often do you get seemingly crazy ideas which, on further development, turn out to be good and useful? |
| 9. Mental agility | —How good are you at coping with several problems or tasks at the same time?<br>—Can you think of a few examples of situations in which you really needed to think quickly? What happened in each case?<br>—How often do you get sudden flashes of insight, in which 'all the pieces seem to come together' to solve a problem? Can you think of some examples of this?<br>—How do you feel when faced with the need for rapid thinking?<br>—What do you do when faced with seemingly contradictory information, data, or ideas? |

*Table 5.1 continued*

| Quality | Indicative questions |
|---------|----------------------|
| 10. Balanced learning habits and skills | —How good are you at relating theory and practice in management?<br>—Can you think of examples of occasions when you were able to draw general conclusions, or generate mini-theories, from your own practical experiences?<br>—Can you think of examples of occasions on which you<br>    (a) preferred to rely on the guidance of an expert rather than trust your own judgement? and<br>    (b) preferred to trust your own judgement rather than rely on the guidance of an expert?<br>—What do you do to ensure that you use a balanced range of learning habits? |
| 11. Self-knowledge | —What do you do to increase your level of self-knowledge?<br>—Can you give examples of instances when knowledge or understanding of how you were feeling or behaving affected what you were doing?<br>—To what extent are you consciously aware of your own goals, values, beliefs, feelings, behaviour?<br>—How often do you stop to consider your own behaviour, its causes and its effects? |

*Table 5.1 continued*

31

| 1 Qualities of effective managers | 2 First self-rating | 3 1st goals | 4 Second self-rating | 5 2nd goals | 6 Third self-rating | 7 3rd goals |
|---|---|---|---|---|---|---|
| | Today's date is _____ | | Today's date is _____ | | Today's date is _____ | |
| 1. Command of basic facts | 1. My command of basic facts is quite satisfactory<br>2. My command of basic facts is quite good, but should be a little greater<br>3. My command of basic facts is not good, and should be much greater<br>4. My command of basic facts is very poor, and should be very much greater | | 1. My command of basic facts is quite satisfactory<br>2. My command of basic facts is quite good, but should be a little greater<br>3. My command of basic facts is not good, and should be much greater<br>4. My command of basic facts is very poor, and should be very much greater | | 1. My command of basic facts is quite satisfactory<br>2. My command of basic facts is quite good, but should be a little greater<br>3. My command of basic facts is not good, and should be much greater<br>4. My command of basic facts is very poor, and should be very much greater | |
| 2. Relevant professional knowledge | 1. My level of relevant professional knowledge is quite satisfactory<br>2. My level of relevant professional knowledge is quite good, but should be a little greater<br>3. My level of relevant professional knowledge is not good, and should be much greater | | 1. My level of relevant professional knowledge is quite satisfactory<br>2. My level of relevant professional knowledge is quite good, but should be a little greater<br>3. My level of relevant professional knowledge is not good, and should be much greater | | 1. My level of relevant professional knowledge is quite satisfactory<br>2. My level of relevant professional knowledge is quite good, but should be a little greater<br>3. My level of relevant professional knowledge is not good, and should be much greater | |

*Table 5.2. For use with self-diagnosis Methods One and Two; simple introspection and conversation with a partner.*

| 1<br>Qualities of effective managers | 2<br>First self-rating | 3<br>1st goals | 4<br>Second self-rating | 5<br>2nd goals | 6<br>Third self-rating | 7<br>3rd goals |
|---|---|---|---|---|---|---|
| | Today's date is ___<br>4. My level of relevant professional knowledge is very poor, and should be very much greater | | Today's date is ___<br>4. My level of relevant professional knowledge is very poor, and should be very much greater | | Today's date is ___<br>4. My level of relevant professional knowledge is very poor, and should be very much greater | |
| 3. Continuing sensitivity to events | 1. My sensitivity to events is quite satisfactory<br>2. My sensitivity to events is quite good, but should be a little greater<br>3. My sensitivity to events is not good, and should be much greater<br>4. My sensitivity to events is very poor, and should be very much greater | | 1. My sensitivity to events is quite satisfactory<br>2. My sensitivity to events is quite good, but should be a little greater<br>3. My sensitivity to events is not good, and should be much greater<br>4. My sensitivity to events is very poor, and should be very much greater | | 1. My sensitivity to events is quite satisfactory<br>2. My sensitivity to events is quite good, but should be a little greater<br>3. My sensitivity to events is not good, and should be much greater<br>4. My sensitivity to events is very poor, and should be very much greater | |
| 4. Problem-solving, analytical, and decision/judgement-making skills | 1. My level of these skills is quite satisfactory<br>2. My level of these skills is quite good, but should be a little greater | | 1. My level of these skills is quite satisfactory<br>2. My level of these skills is quite good, but should be a little greater | | 1. My level of these skills is quite satisfactory<br>2. My level of these skills is quite good, but should be a little greater | |

Table 5.2. continued

| 1<br>Qualities of effective managers | 2<br>First self-rating | 3<br>1st goals | 4<br>Second self-rating | 5<br>2nd goals | 6<br>Third self-rating | 7<br>3rd goals |
|---|---|---|---|---|---|---|
| | Today's date is ____<br><br>3. My level of these skills is not good, and should be much greater<br>4. My level of these skills is very poor, and should be very much greater | | Today's date is ____<br><br>3. My level of these skills is not good, and should be much greater<br>4. My level of these skills is very poor, and should be very much greater | | Today's date is ____<br><br>3. My level of these skills is not good, and should be much greater<br>4. My level of these skills is very poor, and should be very much greater | |
| 5. Social skills and abilities | 1. My level of social skills is quite satisfactory<br>2. My level of social skills is quite good, but should be a little greater<br>3. My level of social skills is not good, and should be much greater<br>4. My level of social skills is very poor, and should be very much greater | | 1. My level of social skills is quite satisfactory<br>2. My level of social skills is quite good, but should be a little greater<br>3. My level of social skills is not good, and should be much greater<br>4. My level of social skills is very poor, and should be very much greater | | 1. My level of social skills is quite satisfactory<br>2. My level of social skills is quite good, but should be a little greater<br>3. My level of social skills is not good, and should be much greater<br>4. My level of social skills is very poor, and should be very much greater | |
| 6. Emotional resilience | 1. My level of emotional resilience is quite satisfactory | | 1. My level of emotional resilience is quite satisfactory | | 1. My level of emotional resilience is quite satisfactory | |

Table 5.2. continued

| 1 Qualities of effective managers | 2 First self-rating | 3 1st goals | 4 Second self-rating | 5 2nd goals | 6 Third self-rating | 7 3rd goals |
|---|---|---|---|---|---|---|
| | Today's date is ___ | | Today's date is ___ | | Today's date is ___ | |
| | 2. My level of emotional resilience is quite good, but should be a little greater<br>3. My level of emotional resilience is not good, and should be much greater<br>4. My level of emotional resilience is very poor, and should be very much greater | | 2. My level of emotional resilience is quite good, but should be a little greater<br>3. My level of emotional resilience is not good, and should be much greater<br>4. My level of emotional resilience is very poor, and should be very much greater | | 2. My level of emotional resilience is quite good, but should be a little greater<br>3. My level of emotional resilience is not good, and should be much greater<br>4. My level of emotional resilience is very poor, and should be very much greater | |
| 7. Proactivity— inclination to respond purposefully to events | 1. My level of proactivity is quite satisfactory<br>2. My level of proactivity is quite good, but should be a little greater<br>3. My level of proactivity is not good, and should be much greater<br>4. My level of proactivity is very poor, and should be very much greater | | 1. My level of proactivity is quite satisfactory<br>2. My level of proactivity is quite good, but should be a little greater<br>3. My level of proactivity is not good, and should be much greater<br>4. My level of proactivity is very poor, and should be very much greater | | 1. My level of proactivity is quite satisfactory<br>2. My level of proactivity is quite good, but should be a little greater<br>3. My level of proactivity is not good, and should be much greater<br>4. My level of proactivity is very poor, and should be very much greater | |

Table 5.2. continued

35

| 1<br>Qualities of effective managers | 2<br>First self-rating | 3<br>1st goals | 4<br>Second self-rating | 5<br>2nd goals | 6<br>Third self-rating | 7<br>3rd goals |
|---|---|---|---|---|---|---|
| | Today's date is ____ | | Today's date is ____ | | Today's date is ____ | |
| 8. Creativity | 1. My level of creativity is quite satisfactory<br>2. My level of creativity is quite good, but should be a little greater<br>3. My level of creativity is not good, and should be much greater<br>4. My level of creativity is very poor, and should be very much greater | | 1. My level of creativity is quite satisfactory<br>2. My level of creativity is quite good, but should be a little greater<br>3. My level of creativity is not good, and should be much greater<br>4. My level of creativity is very poor, and should be very much greater | | 1. My level of creativity is quite satisfactory<br>2. My level of creativity is quite good, but should be a little greater<br>3. My level of creativity is not good, and should be much greater<br>4. My level of creativity is very poor, and should be very much greater | |
| 9. Mental agility | 1. My level of mental agility is quite satisfactory<br>2. My level of mental agility is quite good, but should be a little greater<br>3. My level of mental agility is not good, and should be much greater<br>4. My level of mental agility is very poor, and should be very much greater | | 1. My level of mental agility is quite satisfactory<br>2. My level of mental agility is quite good, but should be a little greater<br>3. My level of mental agility is not good, and should be much greater<br>4. My level of mental agility is very poor, and should be very much greater | | 1. My level of mental agility is quite satisfactory<br>2. My level of mental agility is quite good, but should be a little greater<br>3. My level of mental agility is not good, and should be much greater<br>4. My level of mental agility is very poor, and should be very much greater | |

*Table 5.2. continued*

| 1<br>Qualities of effective managers | 2<br>First self-rating | 3<br>1st goals | 4<br>Second self-rating | 5<br>2nd goals | 6<br>Third self-rating | 7<br>3rd goals |
|---|---|---|---|---|---|---|
| | Today's date is ___ | | Today's date is ___ | | Today's date is ___ | |
| 10. Balanced learning habits and skills | 1. The balance of my learning habits and skills is quite satisfactory<br>2. The balance of my learning habits and skills is quite good, but should be a little better<br>3. The balance of my learning habits and skills is not good, and should be much better<br>4. The balance of my learning habits and skills is very poor, and should be much better | | 1. The balance of my learning habits and skills is quite satisfactory<br>2. The balance of my learning habits and skills is quite good, but should be a little better<br>3. The balance of my learning habits and skills is not good, and should be much better<br>4. The balance of my learning habits and skills is very poor, and should be very much better | | 1. The balance of my learning habits and skills is quite satisfactory<br>2. The balance of my learning habits and skills is quite good, but should be a little better<br>3. The balance of my learning habits and skills is not good, and should be much better<br>4. The balance of my learning habits and skills is very poor, and should be very much better | |
| 11. Self-knowledge | 1. The level of my self-knowledge is quite satisfactory<br>2. The level of my self-knowledge is quite good, but should be a little greater | | 1. The level of my self-knowledge is quite satisfactory<br>2. The level of my self-knowledge is quite good, but should be a little greater | | 1. The level of my self-knowledge is quite satisfactory<br>2. The level of my self-knowledge is quite good, but should be a little greater | |

Table 5.2 continued

| 1<br>Qualities of effective managers | 2<br>First self-rating | 3<br>1st goals | 4<br>Second self-rating | 5<br>2nd goals | 6<br>Third self-rating | 7<br>3rd goals |
|---|---|---|---|---|---|---|
| | Today's date<br><br>is _____ | | Today's date<br><br>is _____ | | Today's date<br><br>is _____ | |
| | 3. The level of my self-knowledge is not good, and should be much greater<br>4. The level of my self-knowledge is very poor, and should be very much greater | | 3. The level of my self-knowledge is not good, and should be much greater<br>4. The level of my self-knowledge is very poor, and should be very much greater | | 3. The level of my self-knowledge is not good, and should be much greater<br>4. The level of my self-knowledge is very poor, and should be very much greater | |

*Table 5.2. continued*

*Step 2. Goal setting*

Look over your answers. Do any areas stand out in which you feel you are particularly lacking in skills or abilities? Or are your scores more or less the same for each of the 11 qualities?

If one or two stand out clearly, choose these as your first priorities. If they are all more or less the same, select a couple either at random, or which particularly appeal to you.

However you choose them, concentrate on one or two areas only. You can come back to the others later.

When you have chosen your one or two priority areas, these can be indicated in column 3 of Table 5.2—'1st goals'. Give yourself a specific goal; for example:

'By                    (choose a realistic date by which you hope to have achieved this goal) I will have carried out all (or 50 per cent or whatever) of the activities, provided that they are related to this goal area.'*

OR

'By                    (date) I will have increased my self-rating in this goal area from                    (rating now) to
(target rating),

*Step 3.  Planning for on-going evaluation*

It is important to recognize that self-development must be a continuous process. For this reason, the activities presented in Part 2 of this book are designed so that most of them can become incorporated into your everyday way of doing things.

Review your progress and set new goals as time proceeds. When your target date (i.e., the date you have indicated in column 3) arrives, you should then complete column 4 of Table 5.2, recommencing the self-diagnosis procedure, which thus becomes a cycle:

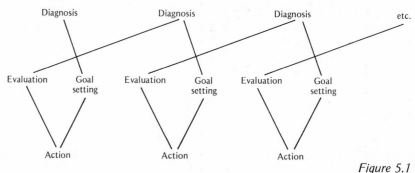

*Figure 5.1*

* Chapter 6 provides a means of identifying which activities are related to which goal areas.

It is, of course, important to be honest with yourself when diagnosing your needs; since there are no points to be scored or exams to be passed, the only person you will be cheating if you are not honest will be yourself. The value of this book is very much determined by *your* commitment—commitment to self-honesty and to action.

When you have completed column 4, you can then continue with new goals (column 5) and, in due course, further self-ratings, goals, self-ratings, goals, etc., *ad infinitum*. We use this phrase advisedly, since the ideal is that you incorporate this way of thinking, diagnosing, and goal setting into your everyday activities as a manager, hence, increasing your effectiveness.

### Method two: conversation with a partner

Although this book is designed so that you can work through it on your own, it will be helpful to work with somebody else. An appropriate partner may give useful feedback, challenge assumptions, provide support, help sound out ideas.

The partner must be committed to the role. An ideal situation would be one in which you and a colleague both undertake a programme of self-development, so that you can each act as helper to the other.

For those who are able to work with a partner, we present this second method of self-diagnosis and goal setting. In essence it is the same as Method One, with the additional factor that you discuss each step with your partner.

*Step 1. Diagnosis*

Column 1 of Table 5.2 lists the 11 qualities of the effective manager. Take each quality in turn and discuss it with your partner. Ask yourselves how well equipped you are in each case. How much of the quality do you possess, and to what extent would you like to develop it further? Use the indicative questions given in Table 5.1. Think about these questions, ask your partner for views on your attributes, compare his views with your own and, if necessary, think again and explore further. When you think you have really examined yourself indicate your conclusions by circling 1, 2, 3, or 4 in column 2 of Table 5.2.

*Step 2. Goal setting*

This is as Step 2 in Method One—but again, work with your partner by sharing your conclusions and goals.

*Step 3. Planning for on-going evaluation*

Again, this is as in Method One (Step 3), but is done collaboratively, with your partner.

## Method three: self-administered questionnaire

The first two methods have been relatively open-ended. They required you to think, in only a semistructured way, about yourself in relation to the qualities of an effective manager, and then rate yourself on a four-point scale.

The third method is more structured in that it uses a specific set of questions, with a predetermined scoring scheme.

*Step 1.  Diagnosis*

The questionnaire below contains 110 questions. Table 5.3 is designed as a means of scoring your answers to the questionnaire.

For each of the 110 statements, you tick or circle, in the respective cell or box of Table 5.3 (a), (b), (c), or (d). The answer scheme is:

(a) Mark (a) if you think that the statement is *definitely not true* of you; you *strongly disagree* with the statement; you *never behave or feel* the way indicated by the statement.

(b) Mark (b) if you think that the statement is *sometimes true* of you; you *partly agree* with the statement; you *sometimes behave or feel* the way indicated by the statement.

(c) Mark (c) if you think that the statement is *generally true* of you; you *definitely agree* with the statement; you *quite often behave or feel* the way indicated by the statement.

(d) Mark (d) if you think that the statement is *always, or very nearly always*, true of you; you *strongly agree* with the statement; you *usually or always behave or feel* the way indicated by the statement.

Instructions for calculating your results are given after Table 5.3.

## THE QUESTIONNAIRE

1. I find I don't know enough about what's going on around me.
2. I find that I don't know enough about the technical aspects of my job.
3. I don't seem able to pick up quickly what's going on.
4. I dither when faced with a decision.
5. I find that other people don't listen to me properly.
6. I try to be objective and not to worry about my feelings.

7. I respond to the pressures of the instant, thus losing sight of longer-term considerations.

8. I find it difficult to come up with new ideas.

9. Compared with other people, I'm rather slow on the uptake.

10. I don't see much connection between theory and practice in management.

11. I find it difficult to ask other people what they really think of me.

12. I make plans or decisions only to find later on that they are no longer valid because of something that I should have known but didn't.

13. Many of the people working with or for me seem to know more about various aspects of the job than I do.

14. I'm not very good at knowing or recognizing what other people are thinking or feeling.

15. I have difficulty in analysing a situation into its various aspects.

16. There are times when I just don't seem to be able to get other people to see my point of view.

17. I get worried because there's no way of knowing in advance whether or not I have made the right decision.

18. I find that after a while there's no point in keeping up a losing struggle.

19. I'm not an imaginative person.

20. I have difficulty in thinking on my feet in tricky situations.

21. Experience is the only valid teacher.

22. It's dangerous to be introspective.

23. I get caught out because I don't know what's happening in my organization.

24. I would like to be more up-to-date on the technical aspects of my job.

25. I find that when something happens I'm only aware of part of what's going on—I overlook other aspects of the situation or problem.

26. I find it difficult to weigh up the pros and cons of a solution to a problem.

27. Anger and conflict tend to frighten or upset me.

28. I have difficulty in sleeping at night.

29. It's difficult to think very far ahead, since the immediate goal is more important.

30. I don't think that people with other specialist interests have much to offer me in my particular job.

31. I prefer to work on one thing at a time rather than be dealing with several things at once.

32. I'm not able to convert my own experiences into valid theories.

33. There's just not enough time in my job to sit around talking about how we feel about each other.

34. People don't seem to tell me enough about what's going on in the organization.
35. It would help me in my job if I could learn more about relevant techniques.
36. Other people seem to notice more than I do about what's happening around them.
37. I tend to jump to instant conclusions—acting quickly without spending much time thinking.
38. I avoid telling people what I really think about them.
39. When I'm nervous or tired I snap at people or get moody and irritable.
40. I'm passive rather than active.
41. My job is unique, so I don't think that people from other backgrounds could be of much help to me.
42. Once I get stuck into a task I try to remain with it rather than switch to something else and then back again.
43. I don't sit and think abstract thoughts about management.
44. I'm basically a logical person, and I don't let my feelings influence me.
45. I find that I need more information about the organization but don't know how to get it.
46. I am not very well versed in the range of techniques that could be relevant to my job.
47. I don't really feel tuned-in to what's happening in a situation.
48. I find it difficult to trust my own judgement.
49. I find myself irritated by other people.
50. I don't think that feelings should be brought into issues.
51. I need to temper initiative with caution.
52. I am better at implementing well-tried solutions rather than experimenting with new ones.
53. To see the whole situation one must carefully consider all the parts.
54. It's best to rely on experts when seeking ideas about specialized aspects of one's job.
55. I don't think we should let our values and feelings affect the way we behave at work.
56. I don't have a clear understanding of how my organization works.
57. I would like to have more theoretical knowledge that would help me in my job.
58. I have difficulty in knowing what other people are up to.
59. Having made up my mind about something I like to get somebody else's opinion about my decision.
60. I don't really know what others think of me.

61. I don't get emotional in my job—I just stick to the facts.

62. I find it difficult to stick at it when things aren't going too well.

63. I get mental blockages when trying to think of new ways of doing things.

64. 'Slow and steady wins the race' is a pretty good motto.

65. When I get an idea I like, if possible, to have it checked out by an expert.

66. My medium- and long-term ambitions are not clear.

67. I have difficulty in getting all the information I need.

68. I find that I don't seem to know enough about external factors such as market changes, new legislation, and the like.

69. I find myself surprised because I've only been seeing 'part of the picture'.

70. I would like some sort of a formula that I could apply to problems so as to work out the best solution or decision.

71. I usually lose arguments.

72. I find myself aware that I'm behaving inappropriately, but don't seem to be able to stop or change the way I'm acting.

73. I feel a need to have more 'get-up-and-go'.

74. I have difficulty in coming up with new ideas.

75. I can't cope with more than one or two problems at a time.

76. If I go on a course I would like the teachers or trainers to be able to give me a lot of information and ideas.

77. There's not much point in thinking about oneself and 'contemplating one's navel'.

78. Many of my colleagues seem to know more about the organization than I do.

79. I have difficulty in keeping up with new techniques and developments.

80. If somebody changed their hair-style, or the way they dressed, I probably wouldn't notice.

81. I get confused when faced with several alternative courses of action.

82. I don't really see it as part of my job to step in between two people who don't get on with each other, as long as they do their job satisfactorily.

83. I worry about problems over and over in my mind.

84. If forced to choose between two descriptions of myself, I would say that I am steady and reliable rather than adventurous and risk taking.

85. Other people seem better than me at thinking of new ways of solving problems.

86. I'm not what you'd call a quick thinker.

87. If I hear of a new theory I find it difficult to translate it into practical terms relevant to my job.
88. I wouldn't like other people to tell me exactly what they think of me.
89. I don't really know who the important people are in my organization.
90. I would welcome the opportunity to learn more about the theoretical background to my job.
91. I have difficulty in knowing how other people are feeling.
92. When trying to make a decision I find that I've got so much information that I don't know what to do with it.
93. I find that I simply cannot understand why someone else feels the way he does.
94. I don't discuss my feelings or worries with other people.
95. I prefer to follow someone else's plans or instructions rather than act on my own initiative.
96. I don't seem as good as other people at getting creative ideas.
97. The trouble with my job is that I'm never left alone to get on with it—there are too many interruptions.
98. I dislike jargon or over-theoretical ways of talking.
99. It's a good job we can't read the thoughts of others.
100. I would like to know more about my organization's policies and future plans.
101. I am not really sufficiently *au fait* with the technical requirements of my job.
102. I find myself surprised at the way other people react to what's happening.
103. I tend to find that I can't make a decision because I don't have enough relevant information.
104. Many of the people in my organization can't be trusted to get on with their job without constant supervision.
105. Most days I wake up with a 'Monday-morning' feeling.
106. It's better to be safe than sorry.
107. Compared with other people, my ideas seem to be stuck in a rut, or fixed by well-established ways of doing things.
108. When I'm under pressure, in a tight spot, or being challenged, I can't seem to think straight or express my ideas clearly.
109. I'm the sort of person who goes around saying 'no one can tell me how to do my job'.
110. I don't spend much time thinking about myself—my strengths and weaknesses.

| | | | | | | | | | | |
|---|---|---|---|---|---|---|---|---|---|---|
| 1 a b c d | 2 a b c d | 3 a b c d | 4 a b c d | 5 a b c d | 6 a b c d | 7 a b c d | 8 a b c d | 9 a b c d | 10 a b c d | 11 a b c d |
| 12 a b c d | 13 a b c d | 14 a b c d | 15 a b c d | 16 a b c d | 17 a b c d | 18 a b c d | 19 a b c d | 20 a b c d | 21 a b c d | 22 a b c d |
| 23 a b c d | 24 a b c d | 25 a b c d | 26 a b c d | 27 a b c d | 28 a b c d | 29 a b c d | 30 a b c d | 31 a b c d | 32 a b c d | 33 a b c d |
| 34 a b c d | 35 a b c d | 36 a b c d | 37 a b c d | 38 a b c d | 39 a b c d | 40 a b c d | 41 a b c d | 42 a b c d | 43 a b c d | 44 a b c d |
| 45 a b c d | 46 a b c d | 47 a b c d | 48 a b c d | 49 a b c d | 50 a b c d | 51 a b c d | 52 a b c d | 53 a b c d | 54 a b c d | 55 a b c d |
| 56 a b c d | 57 a b c d | 58 a b c d | 59 a b c d | 60 a b c d | 61 a b c d | 62 a b c d | 63 a b c d | 64 a b c d | 65 a b c d | 66 a b c d |
| 67 a b c d | 68 a b c d | 69 a b c d | 70 a b c d | 71 a b c d | 72 a b c d | 73 a b c d | 74 a b c d | 75 a b c d | 76 a b c d | 77 a b c d |
| 78 a b c d | 79 a b c d | 80 a b c d | 81 a b c d | 82 a b c d | 83 a b c d | 84 a b c d | 85 a b c d | 86 a b c d | 87 a b c d | 88 a b c d |
| 89 a b c d | 90 a b c d | 91 a b c d | 92 a b c d | 93 a b c d | 94 a b c d | 95 a b c d | 96 a b c d | 97 a b c d | 98 a b c d | 99 a b c d |
| 100 a b c d | 101 a b c d | 102 a b c d | 103 a b c d | 104 a b c d | 105 a b c d | 106 a b c d | 107 a b c d | 108 a b c d | 109 a b c d | 110 a b c d |
| A | B | C | D | E | F | G | H | I | J | K |

*Table 5.3. For use with self-diagnosis Method Three: self-administered questionnaire*

## SCORING THE QUESTIONNAIRE

To calculate your score, take the first *column* of Table 5.3 (i.e., squares corresponding to questions 1, 12, 23, 34, 45, 56, 67, 78, 89, and 100) and give yourself points as follows:

### 2 points for every (a) marked*

* Although, in theory, an 'a' should incur no points—as it implies no fault or even perfection—it does in fact score 2. The reason being that if you really do come up to 'a' standard you don't need this book; if you don't then you're blind to your faults by putting 'a''s down.

> 1 point for every (b) marked
> 2 points for every (c) marked
> 3 points for every (d) marked

Then add up the total number of points scored in column 1, and write this in the space marked 'A' at the foot of the column.

This procedure should then be repeated for each of the other columns, with totals written in spaces B to K.

The 11 columns (and spaces A to K) correspond to the 11 qualities of an effective manager. The questionnaire is written in such a way that the higher your score, the greater you seem to have a self-development need in respect of that quality.

### Step 2.   Goal setting

First, transfer your scores from Table 5.3 to column 1 of Table 5.4. When you have done this, look over your scores. Are there any that stand out as being higher than others, or are they all more or less the same?

If one or two are definitely higher than others, then it would probably be a good idea to choose these as your priorities to start on. If they are all about the same, however, then you might as well choose one or two either at random or by selecting areas that particularly appeal to you.

In any case, we suggest that at this stage you concentrate on one or two areas only; you can come back to the others later.

When you have chosen your one or two priority areas, these can be indicated in column 3 of Table 5.2—'1st goals'. Try to give yourself a reasonably specific goal, for example:

> 'By               (choose a realistic date by which you hope to have achieved this goal) I will have carried out all (or 50 per cent, or whatever) the activities provided that are related to this goal area.'*

### Step 3.   Planning for on-going evaluation

Review your progress and set new goals as time proceeds. For example, even if you have carried out all the activities related to a particular goal area once, you might wish to do them again. Indeed, many of the activities are such that they can be incorporated into your everyday way of doing your job. Columns 5 and 7 of Table 5.4 are provided to help with this continuous process of goal setting, while columns 4 and 6 provide you with the opportunity to review your progress.

* Chapter 6 provides a means of identifying which activities are related to each particular goal area.

| 1 Score from Table 5.3 | 2 Corresponding quality of effective manager | 3 1st goals Today's date is ___ | 4 Progress review Date ___ | 5 2nd goals Today's date is ___ | 6 Progress review Date ___ | 7 3rd goals Today's date is ___ |
|---|---|---|---|---|---|---|
| A: | 1. Command of basic facts | | | | | |
| B: | 2. Relevant professional knowledge and understanding | | | | | |
| C: | 3. Continuing sensitivity to events | | | | | |
| D: | 4. Problem solving, analytical, and decision/judgement-making skills | | | | | |
| E: | 5. Social skills and abilities | | | | | |
| F: | 6. Emotional resilience | | | | | |
| G: | 7. Proactivity— inclination to respond purposefully to events | | | | | |
| H: | 8. Creativity | | | | | |
| I: | 9. Mental agility | | | | | |
| J: | 10. Balanced learning habits and skills | | | | | |
| K: | 11. Self-knowledge | | | | | |

*Table 5.4. For use with self-diagnosis Method Three: self-administered questionnaire*

CONCLUSION

In this chapter we have described three different ways in which you can diagnose your own self-development needs and set some appropriate goals.

In Part 2 we present a number of activities that will help you in achieving these goals. In chapter 6 we give a guide to selecting activities for the development of each of the 11 qualities of the effective manager, followed by a chart which relates the activities to the particular qualities. Chapter 7 gives some general guidelines on the use of the activities, which are contained in Part 2.

# 6. A guide to the selection of activities

By now you will have set yourself some learning goals for self-development. This brief chapter is about how you select some of the 'activities' set out in the remaining part of the book.

Table 6.1 shows down one side the 11 areas of learning, and along the top the name and number of each of the 39 activities provided for you in this book. We have put a large cross in the column for each learning area against each activity which is designed to bring about *major learning* in that area. We have put small crosses where we believe that there is some payoff from the activity, although it is not primarily designed for learning in the area covered.

By going down the columns of the learning areas which are priorities for you, you can begin to choose activities which should be relevant to you.

You will need an approach to decide the order in which to tackle activities. Here are three possibilities:

1. You will remember that four of the learning areas: self-knowledge, balanced learning habits, mental agility, and creativity, are thought to be important to managers because they allow them to quickly develop and use the other more specific skills and qualities. One strategy is for you to start with any learning goals you may have in these areas, because it makes sense to start with activities which help you 'learn to learn'. This will help you get the most out of subsequent activities.

2. Another possibility, appropriate if your time is limited or if the problems that you want to learn to cope with are pressing, is to start with your most urgent learning goals, the ones that you have concluded are your greatest area of weakness.

3. You could begin by trying one or two of the activities, and make up your mind what to do next as you go along. This will allow you to get a feel for the kind of activities that suit you. We expect that some of the activities will work for you better than others and that these will not necessarily be the same as those that work, or do not work, for other people.

| ACTIVITIES / LEARNING AREA | 1. Extend your knowledge of situational facts | 2. Making contacts | 3. Managing your time | 4. Keeping up-to-date | 5. Facts and assumptions | 6. Personal journal | 7. Decision making | 8. Planning + decision-making techniques | 9. Choosing solutions with a chance | 10. Role set analysis | 11. Planning change | 12. Analysis of experiences | 13. Catastrophic contingencies | 14. Scheduling | 15. Budgetary control | 16. Response to conflict | 17. Practising new group behaviour | 18. Interpreting yourself and others | 19. Counselling style inventory | 20. Getting to know you | 21. Relaxation | 22. Fitness | 23. Managing your feelings | 24. Stability zones | 25. Who's the boss? | 26. Practising change | 27. Action planning | 28. Accepting other people's ideas | 29. Brainstorming | 30. Approaches to creativity | 31. Attribute alternatives | 32. Coping with complexity | 33. Quick thinking | 34. Developing a helicopter mind | 35. Managing your dependency | 36. Understanding your learning processes | 37. Study skills | 38. How do you learn? | 39. Conversations with yourself |
|---|---|---|---|---|---|---|---|---|---|---|---|---|---|---|---|---|---|---|---|---|---|---|---|---|---|---|---|---|---|---|---|---|---|---|---|---|---|---|---|
| Situational facts | X | X |  |  |  |  |  |  |  | X |  |  |  |  |  |  |  |  |  |  |  |  |  |  |  |  |  |  |  |  |  |  |  |  |  |  |  |  |  |
| Professional knowledge | X | X |  | X |  |  | X |  |  |  |  |  | X | X |  |  |  |  |  |  |  |  |  |  |  |  |  |  |  |  |  |  |  |  |  | X | X |  |  |
| Sensitivity to events | X |  | X | X | X |  |  |  |  |  |  |  |  |  |  |  |  |  |  |  |  |  |  |  |  |  |  |  |  |  |  |  |  |  | X |  |  |  |  |
| Analytical skills |  |  |  | X | X | X | X | X | X | X | X | X | X | X | X | X |  | X |  |  |  |  |  | X | X | X | X |  |  |  |  | X |  |  |  |  | X |  |  |
| Social skills |  | X |  |  | X |  |  | X | X |  |  |  |  |  |  | X | X | X | X |  |  |  |  |  |  |  |  | X |  |  |  |  |  |  |  |  |  |  |  |
| Emotional resilience |  |  |  |  |  |  |  |  |  |  |  |  |  |  | X | X | X |  | X | X | X | X | X | X | X | X |  |  |  |  | X |  |  |  |  |  |  |  |  |
| Proactivity | X |  |  |  |  |  |  |  | X | X |  | X |  |  | X | X |  |  |  |  |  |  |  |  | X | X |  |  |  |  |  |  |  |  |  |  |  |  |  |
| Creativity |  |  |  |  |  |  |  |  |  |  |  | X |  |  |  |  |  |  |  |  |  | X |  |  |  |  | X | X | X | X |  | X | X |  |  |  |  |  |  |
| Mental agility |  |  |  |  |  |  |  |  |  |  |  |  |  |  |  |  |  |  |  |  |  |  |  |  |  |  |  |  |  | X | X | X | X | X |  |  |  |  |  |
| Balanced learning habits |  |  | X |  | X |  |  |  |  |  | X |  |  |  |  |  |  |  |  |  |  |  |  |  |  |  |  |  |  |  |  |  |  |  | X | X | X | X |  |
| Self-knowledge |  |  |  |  | X | X |  |  |  |  |  | X |  |  |  |  | X | X | X |  |  |  |  |  |  |  | X |  |  |  |  |  |  | X | X | X | X | X | X |

Table 6.1.  Activities/learning areas matrix

# 7. How to use the activities

One point before you start on the activities: there are many paths to self-development and the approach offered in this book is just one. Through learner control and responsibility, management self-development takes many guises. Some of those most commonly found within organizations are

- —coaching/counselling;
- —appraisal,
- —internal rotation, attachment, and placement;
- —external attachments and placements;
- —reading;
- —committee membership;
- —discussion groups, working parties, meetings of professional bodies and institutes;
- —learning from one's own job and experience;
- —special activities.

This book represents one example of the last two categories in the list. Many of the experiences listed do not lead to development or learning. They either take predictable routine courses, such as in committees or professional-body gatherings, or they are used too frequently as control rather than development mechanisms, such as in personnel appraisal. This need not be so. With effort on the part of the manager involved, most of the experiences can become enriching and rewarding. We recommend that you scan all of the self-development opportunities open to you and take advantage of some of them.

First, though, the main purpose of this book is to provide you with a number of activities or exercises which you can use as part of your self-development programme. Here are a few notes which we hope will help you to get the most out of them.

*Commitment*

There is no point in cheating. Just as exercises for physical fitness are of no use if you only pretend to do them, or do them half-heartedly, so with the mental exercises in this book. The more you put into them, the more you will get out of them.

### Working with a partner

The activities can all be done on your own, but even more benefit can be obtained through working with a partner. It doesn't matter *who* the partner is (colleague, friend, spouse), but it is important *what* he or she is. The partner should be someone you can trust and who will help by providing you with honest feedback and by being a good, challenging listener. Ideally, each of you should undertake to help the other so that, as well as helping, each is being helped. Working with a partner can also increase commitment to the programme.

If you decide to work with a partner, 'Getting to Know You' (Activity 20) provides an opportunity to build a useful helping relationship.

### Working with support groups

This involved a number—say 8 to 12—managers agreeing to try out the activities in their own time. At regular intervals (once or twice a month) they meet for a couple of hours to share experiences and help each other by discussion, giving feedback, and support. Your personnel or training manager might help if you want to set up such a group in your own organization. Alternatively, ask your local college of further education or polytechnic if they would set up a support group as part of their management education programme. Finally, the authors will be pleased to give information and advice on support groups in your area.

## When and where?

A number of the activities are such that you will have little choice of location; others can be done wherever you like.

Obviously you need a time and place where you will be free from interruption. You might like to set aside an hour at lunch-time, or in the evening. You might find it possible to do some activities on the train (instead of the crossword puzzle). It really is up to you. However, we suggest that you try to set aside certain specific periods of time, rather than just saying, 'I'll have a go when I get the chance'. Setting aside a particular time is a necessary act of commitment to the self-development programme.

Once you have started work on the activities, they will tend to become incorporated into the way you work.

Doing

Each activity is designed around a three-stage model of learning:

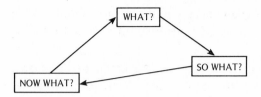

*Figure 7.1. Doing the activities*

*The 'what?' phase*

Basically, this is the experience itself, and your immediate observations. The activities tell you what to do, and ask you to note what happens. It is very important to write down your observations when instructed to do so. Writing is an aid to commitment, helps to clarify what is going on, and serves as a reference for future use.

*The 'so what?' phase*

This consists of thinking about what happened, and noting your reactions to it. These reactions might be feelings, ideas, insights, questions. As time goes on, you might find that at this stage you can see a link between what is happening now and what happened on a previous occasion. This link might be in similarities (of ideas, reactions, or feelings), of changes in yourself, and so on. Again, writing these down is likely to increase the benefits you will gain from the activity.

*The 'now what?' phase*

This is perhaps the most difficult. It consists of taking stock of what you have done and what you have observed, felt, and learned (the 'what?' and 'so what?'), and deciding its significance for you in future action. Thus the 'now what?' phase requires you to make concrete plans for future behaviour based on the insights and developments that the exercise has given you. It is particularly important to try to write these down, since they can then be used as the basis for on-going personal evaluation.

## Incorporation of activities into everyday behaviour

We do not claim that doing each of these activities once will develop you into a perfect manager. Rather, the idea is that by doing the exercises you will start the process of examining yourself in light of the 11 qualities of an effective manager, and start a development process which, if continued, will, we believe, have considerable effect.

Therefore, the aim is to incorporate the ways of behaviour that are established by the activities into your everyday behaviour. You might do this by repeating an activity, possibly with modifications to suit your circumstances. When you have done this a few times, particularly if you notice the various skills and abilities growing as you do so, you should make a conscious effort to turn everyday situations into activities for self-development.

As time goes on, then, you will, we hope, be keeping track of your own progress (Chapter 5 gives some ways of doing this; also Activity 6, 'Personal Journal', can serve this purpose), repeating activities, modifying them, generating your own, and gradually using your own everyday work experiences as opportunities for experimentation, learning, and self-development. When you reach this stage, you will be what someone once called a 'learning manager', and this book will have achieved its purpose.

# Part 2
## Activities for management self-development

Part 2 consists entirely of 39 self-development activities numbered and in the order given in Table 6.1. As we mentioned earlier the sequence is not designed to lead you through from 1 to 39. To get the most out of the exercises you need to develop a learning strategy along the lines suggested in chapter 6.

Although the activities are designed as self-contained units to stand alone or in sequence with others, there is inevitably some overlap. This occurs where it is necessary for the completeness of one particular activity. This has been kept to a minimum, but you will come across some repetition.

To summarize briefly you can work through the activities

- —alone
- —with a partner
- —in a small self-development group

depending upon your situation and your preferred learning style. The extent to which you are able to transfer learning into your job behaviour will depend upon a number of variables other than your own skills and abilities. For example, it depends upon the extent to which you are allowed to try out new ideas by your boss and those in senior positions. It depends on the extent to which your organization encourages new ideas and initiatives. It depends upon the learning climate of your organization.

One final reminder: you are almost certainly someone else's boss. This puts you in a strong position to help and influence the learning and development of your subordinates. How well are you cultivating a good learning climate?

# Activity 1
## Extend your knowledge of situational facts

All the time at work you make decisions and put them into practice. Decisions take facts into account. Facts are an input to a decision. However good your decision-making abilities, your decisions and the actions which follow them will be wrong if they are based on inaccurate information.

We distinguish here between situational and professional facts. Situational facts are things like the price of a commodity, the size of an order book, a customer's delivery deadline. Professional facts are to do with the technology of a production process, or a specialist management area like industrial relations legislation, or financial reporting requirement.

Professional facts are distinct from professional skills and procedures. They are the professional inputs to *managerial* rather than *professional* decisions. The manager of a plant with a sophisticated technology may have a technical background sufficient to make *managerial* decisions; to plan, for instance, the plant's output and manning taking account of the need for maintenance. If the plant breaks down technically, the manager may choose to get involved in the technical/professional search for a solution, but when he does so he is temporarily giving up management and returning to a technical/professional role.

Here we are concerned with professional facts as inputs to managerial decisions, rather than with professional skills in dealing with professional problems.

Situational and professsional facts vary in their permanence, from highly variable—like the price of raw materials and the stock level of finished goods—to relatively permanent ones like the date of annual stocktaking, or the order pattern of a regular customer.

*Reviewing your command of situational and professional facts*

The problem in developing your command of situational and professional facts is likely to be more to do with *identifying* what you need to know than actually getting it. Indeed, once you have identified what you need to know it is probably quite easy to get it. The problem is that, usually, we don't

57

know what we don't know and it is the data in this blind spot that we may really need. Look at the situation as shown in Fig. A1.1.

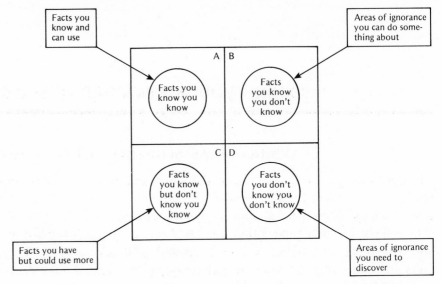

*Figure A1.1*

What you need to do is to convert C's into A's, D's into B's, and B's into A's.

To help with this, we suggest the exercise below which should help you to clarify what you already have in 'A' and 'B', add to it from 'C', and help you explore 'D'.

**Activity**

*Step 1*

Imagine that someone wants to find out whether you are really on the ball on the situational and professional facts concerning your job or occupation. Take a piece of paper and write down as many key questions about such facts of your job as it exists now, and the answers to these questions. Imagine that you have the job of compiling the test questions for a *Mastermind* or *Brain of Britain* TV or radio programme, with your job as the topic.

*Step 2*

Now extend the list of questions and answers by any or all of the following:

(a) If you redesigned, developed, or extended your job in any way that you think desirable, what would this add to the list of questions and answers?

(b) What are the next possible moves in your career—what new facts would you need to have at your command to perform these future jobs?

(c) What kind of training and education are provided for people coming into your kind of work, and your organization? What facts do they have that you haven't?

(d) Imagine showing your list to:

    (i)  your boss;
   (ii)  your subordinates;
  (iii)  your colleagues;
  (iv)  others in similar jobs to yourself;
   (v)  anyone else with whom you are regularly in contact.

What do you think they might suggest that you add to the list?

(e) Show your list to some of the people mentioned in (d) and ask them. Exchange lists with someone in a similar job to yourself who has done this exercise and discuss them both.

(Because of the 'don't-know-what-you-don't-know' factor, second opinions greatly enhance the benefit you can get from this activity. For this reason (e) is particularly important.)

FOLLOW-UP

You probably know the answers to most of the new questions you have posed, but make a list of things you need to know about the others. If any of them are difficult, other activities related to the learning areas 'Sensitivity to Events' and 'Balanced Learning Habits' (Table 6.1) will help you.

# Activity 2
## Making contacts

LEARNING AREAS: SITUATIONAL FACTS: Social skills: Proactivity

The effective manager knows not only 'what's what', but also 'who's who'. He has many contacts within his organization; he knows what other people do, how they relate to his own work, how they can help him, and how he can help them.

**The activity**

The first step is to decide whom you are going to get to know. There are a number of ways of doing this, including:

1. Looking at an organization chart and choosing people in areas about which you know very little.

2. Using an internal telephone directory to the same end.

3. Choosing people in offices around you.

4. Choosing people whom you have seen about the place, without knowing who they are, what they do.

5. Choosing people at random, the third person who enters a lift or walks into the canteen; stick a pin into the internal telephone book.

Having chosen your first potential contact, get to know him. This will be more difficult than it sounds, but less difficult than you imagine. You can explain frankly that you are trying to get to know more people, or, if you prefer a more furtive approach, just try to engage him in informal conversation.

We suggest that your goal should be to find answers to at least the following questions:

(a) What is the person's name?

(b) What is his job title?

(c) What does that job involve?

(d) What does he see as his job's main purpose, its contribution to the organization? Do you agree? If not, can you explore this difference with him?

(e) What are his major goals, concerns, issues, problems?

(f) In what way can he be of help to you?

(g) In what way can you be of help to him?

(h) Are there any ways in which his goals, needs, or interests conflict with yours? If so, what can be done to lessen or overcome this conflict?

You will need to develop certain skills to get the person talking about these things. Some hints on how to do this are given in Table A2.1.

---

1. If you want fairly long, descriptive answers, ask open-ended questions, such as:

   'What ...?'
   'How do you ...?'
   'Could you explain ...?'
   'Can you give an example of ...?'
   'How do you feel about ...?'
   'Why do you ...?'

2. Unless you want very specific, precise, short answers, avoid closed questions, such as:

   'Do you ...?'
   'How often ...?'
   'Is it true that ...?'
   'How many ...?'

3. Notice non-verbal cues, such as tone of voice, changes in posture, facial expression, eye movement, gestures, speech hesitancies.

4. Respond to non-verbal cues by using them to suggest further questions, by remarking on them, or by changing the subject, whichever you think most appropriate.

5. Check out and clarify what you are hearing; that is, repeat in your own words what you think the other person has said, what he means, how he feels.

6. If the other person talks mostly about feelings, it might be useful to ask him about ideas or facts; on the other hand, if he sticks to facts all the time, then try asking him about feelings.

7. From time to time, ask him how he is feeling about you and the process of the discussion.

8. All the time, ask yourself if you are prepared to tell him what you are asking him to tell you.

---

*Table A2.1. Hints on getting another person to talk freely*

FOLLOW-UP

As time goes on you should, using this approach, gradually build an excellent network of contacts throughout the organization. This network will enable you to keep tuned in to what's going on. It will provide you with sources of information, help, and support when needed. In turn, you will be helping others when they need you.

# Activity 3
## Managing your time

LEARNING AREAS: PROFESSIONAL KNOWLEDGE: Situational facts:
Analytical skills

In his book[1] the American social scientist and futurologist, Daniel Bell, talks about and dismisses the concept of post-scarcity society. When most of us think of scarcity, we think of economic scarcity—which Marx blamed for the division of industrial society into classes and which caused Keynes to speculate that if the economic problem were solved, mankind would be deprived of its traditional purpose. Bell points out that scarcity will never disappear, but that old scarcities will be replaced by new ones. New scarcities, like fresh air, open space, and pure water, appear as industry expands to remove the old scarcities. A major scarcity for man in the late twentieth century is time. We will have to budget time as we have budgeted money in the past. There are many reasons for this. Poor, undeveloped societies have time on their hands—there is always tomorrow. In industrial societies, a common characteristic is the careful measurement and allocation of work, but an increasingly common feature is the careful measurement and calculation of leisure time. We have time-saving devices, which paradoxically demand time for maintenance, along with our greatly increased stock of consumer goods. Time is required for our greatly increased capacity to consume and the opportunities for time spending become richer every year. We calculate the opportunity cost of spending time even with friends, relatives, and loved ones.

Make a quick inventory of your free time for the rest of the week:

*Hours*

*Monday*

*Tuesday*

*Wednesday*


*Thursday*


*Friday*


*Saturday*


*Sunday*


Note down for each day how much free time you have. What is left after sleeping, eating, working, travelling? Then try putting down things you could do in this time, under three headings:

1.  Things I MUST do this week:


2.  Things I SHOULD do this week:


3.  Things I would LIKE to do this week:

(if only I had the time)


As this is a private list and for your eyes only, you can afford to be honest with yourself. For example, have you included time for being with close friends and family? Time for doing nothing much? Time to recover from doing too much? Time for passing the time of day with all those other faces and acquaintances in your life?

Peter Drucker[2] pointed out how valuable is this 'free' time—'discretionary time is one of the scarcest and most precious of commodities'. We know the truth of Parkinson's first law: 'Work expands to fill the time available for its completion'. The activity in this section is designed to help you look at how you spend your time at work—although you may wish also to look at how you spend your time out of work. We are concerned primarily with managerial effectiveness and if you feel your outside-work activity is relevant to your job, look at that part of your life too.

A main purpose of the activity is to gain some feeling of control over how your time is spent. This might involve cutting out unnecessary or un-rewarding chunks of time but it might also include looking for chunks of time in which to do things which you're not doing at the moment but which you ought or would like to be doing.

For example, a manager in a large retail company looked at the way he used working time. He discovered that he spent *three hours every day* overseeing and checking the work of subordinates (and another hour each day eating lunch). On top of his own busy job he had subordinates who didn't accept responsibility and who did not exercise initiative. He had a weight problem, because he never had time enough to take exercise. What he could not see was that the way he spent his time was linked to his other problems. How could subordinates exercise responsibility if he gave them no discretion—if their work was continuously checked? He could have gained another half hour by having a light lunch and a walk instead of his usual one-hour three-courser in the management dining room.

So, managing your time properly may increase others' effectiveness and capacity as well as your own. It is also one of the keys to the thorny problem of delegation—are you spending your time on the right activities? We can see you're busy—but doing what?

Managing time is one aspect of managing yourself. One of our characteristics of the effective manager is proactivity: being a self-starter, taking personal responsibility, and getting something done. You can start here.

*Activity*

1. *Recording* how your time is spent.

2. *Analysing* on what you spend your time.

3. *Making decisions* about the most effective use of your discretionary time.

*Step 1*

Before you can manage your time you need to find out what you're doing with it.

Record your activities at work for the next five days. You can design your own recording sheet or use the one given in Table A3.1.

Spend five days at *least* on this—the full value of the exercise cannot be gained from less.

| TIME LOG | | | | |
|---|---|---|---|---|
| Day: _____ Date: _____ | | | | |
| Describe WHAT HAPPENS in detail—the subject of meetings, 'phone calls, letters, reading, conversations. Note the DURATION of each happening. Note the NAME and POSITION of OTHER PEOPLE INVOLVED. Include even casual encounters. | | | | |
| *Time* | *What happened?* | *Duration* | *People involved* | *Comments* |
| 9.00 9.30 | | | | |
| 9.30 10.00 | | | | |
| 10.00 10.30 | | | | |
| 10.30 11.00 | | | | |
| 11.00 11.30 | | | | |
| 11.30 12.00 | | | | |
| 12.00 12.30 | | | | |
| 12.30 1.00 | | | | |
| 1.00 1.30 | | | | |
| 1.30 2.00 | | | | |
| 2.00 2.30 | | | | |
| 2.30 3.00 | | | | |
| 3.00 3.30 | | | | |
| 3.30 4.00 | | | | |
| 4.00 4.30 | | | | |
| 4.30 5.00 | | | | |
| 5.00 5.30 | | | | |

*Table A3.1*

*Step 2*

Analyse your data sheets under a number of headings.

(a) OUTCOME

How successful were the various activities?
Have you any habitual failures?

(b)  TYPE OF WORK

Divide your work tasks into three categories:

  (i)  Things you MUST do?—Your most important duties.
 (ii)  Things you SHOULD do?—Your next most important duties.
(iii)  Things you would LIKE to do?—Your least important duties.

Allocate a theoretical percentage of your effort to each of these, e.g.,

  (i)  75 per cent.
 (ii)  20 per cent.
(iii)  5 per cent.

How much of your time are you spending on each set of activities compared to the 'correct' theoretical mix?

We often concentrate on things we are able to do or like doing at the expense of things which we find difficult. These difficult tasks may be the most vital ones.

Another way of looking at this is to ask yourself what proportion of my time goes on

 (i)  MANAGERIAL WORK—i.e., planning, organizing, motivating.
(ii)  PROFESSIONAL SKILLS—i.e., exercising your old specialist professional skills.

Another common trap is the carrying over of professional work from one's original occupation, e.g., sales, engineering, accounting, into the manager's job. Of course you need to exercise these skills part of the time, but exactly how much is appropriate:

10 per cent?
15 per cent?
20 per cent?

And how much are you *actually* doing?

The *managerial* work may be the most difficult and you may be avoiding it—preferring the comfort of working in your old craft or field.

(c)  WHERE DOES THE WORK COME FROM?

  (i)  Boss —is he delegating enough?
            —is he using you as a personal assistant?
 (ii)  Subordinates—are they too dependent upon you?
(iii)  Self—are you setting yourself enough tasks?
(iv)  Elsewhere —where?
            —how important are these?

### (d) DELEGATION

For each task/happening ask yourself:

 (i) Could this have been delegated?
(ii) If YES, to whom?
  If NO, why not? —your answer to this one should be really thoughtful.
    —is it really your job or have you made yourself indispensable?

You may be able to think of some more headings under which you can analyse your time log.

*Step 3*

After analysis it's time to make some decisions about how to spend your time.

(a) WHAT THINGS ARE YOU SPENDING TIME ON, THAT YOU COULD EITHER CUT OUT, CUT DOWN, OR DELEGATE?

(b) WHAT THINGS ARE YOU NOT DOING NOW THAT YOU SHOULD BE—OR WHAT THINGS SHOULD YOU BE DOING MORE OF?

You can use your three job areas:

 (i) MUST DO
(ii) SHOULD DO
(iii) WOULD LIKE TO

Make sure the MUST DO's are done!

(c) WHAT ACTIONS WILL YOU COMMIT YOURSELF TO HERE AND NOW?

|     | *Action* | *Completed by:* |
|-----|----------|-----------------|
| 1.  |          |                 |
| 2.  |          |                 |
| 3.  |          |                 |
| 4.  |          |                 |
| etc.|          |                 |

## FOLLOW-UP

Obviously you can repeat your time log any time you like to check out how you're functioning, when your best times are, and so on.

If you're interested in reading about how other managers spend their time you might like to look up the following: *Managers and Their Jobs* by Rosemary Stewart (Macmillian, 1967). This book contains data on a large sample of managers gathered from activity and time logs. *The Nature of Managerial Work* by Henry Mintzberg (Harper and Row, 1973).

REFERENCES

1. Bell, D., *The Coming of Post-Industrial Society*, Heinemann, 1974.
2. Drucker, P., *The Effective Executive*, Heinemann, 1967.

# Activity 4
## Keeping up to date

LEARNING AREAS: PROFESSIONAL KNOWLEDGE: Balanced learning habits

Successful managers know what's going on. They are up-to-date on new developments in their areas of professional specialism, and aware of changes and developments in markets, legislation, and so on.

One useful way of keeping up-to-date is by reading the relevant professional journals. Clearly there is a limit to the number of journals one can find the time to read, and each of us will have preferences as to the type of journal we find helpful—some being too theoretical for one person, not theoretical enough for another.

The purpose of this activity is to help you first of all to find out which journals are available in your particular field, and to give you the chance to find out more about these, deciding which ones to read regularly.

**The activity**

*Step 1*

Listed below are a number of particular professional areas. For those areas with which you are concerned, write down the titles of all the relevant journals that you know of.

| | |
|---|---|
| Accountancy | Component Technology |
| Agriculture | Computing |
| Applied Mechanics | Construction |
| Architecture | Control |
| Banking | Corporate Policy |
| Ceramics | Education |
| Chemistry | Electrical Engineering |
| Civil Engineering | Electronics |
| Commerce and Trade | Engineering |
| Communication Technology | Finance |

70

Food Science
Fuel Technology
Hotel and Catering
Industrial Design
Industrial Relations
Iron and Steel
Law
Management
Marketing
Materials Science
Mathematics
Mechanical Engineering

Metallurgy
Mining
Operational Research
Personnel Management
Physics
Power Engineering
Production Engineering
Quality Control
Social Work
Statistics
Structural Engineering
Taxation

*Step 2*

Now compare your list with that given below. Our list is by no means complete—it merely represents some of the journals available in each area and nobody but an unemployed genius would read anything more than a fraction of them. It is designed to show that a considerable number of professional journals exist and we will consider some of them.

*Step 3*

Note some of the journals that are new to you. Choose five or six of these and obtain copies from a library. Your organization may have its own library, and will be able to help you. If it doesn't, check with your public library. The journals may not be in stock, but you have access to the British Library (BL). The public libraries have an obligation to obtain any book or journal held by the BL (which certainly means all the journals listed here, and virtually any book published in the UK or in the USA in recent years). Public libraries tend not to publicize this right of access, so if they seem reluctant to get things for you, remind them of the BL and their obligation to help you (they may make a relatively nominal charge). Libraries in colleges, universities, and polytechnics may also be helpful; if necessary, enrol on a cheap part-time course, which will give you the right of access to the college's library facilities (including obtaining items from the BL).

*Step 4*

Look through the journals and decide which are suitable and which are not. Then make a definite effort to read some of these on a regular basis.

SAMPLE LIST OF JOURNALS

(*Note:* in the following titles, *J.* means *Journal*)

ACCOUNTANCY: *Accountancy; Accountancy and Data Processing Abstract; Accountant; Accounting and Business Research; Accounting Review; Book-keepers J.; Management Accounting; Registered Accountant.*

AGRICULTURE: *ADAS Quarterly Review; Country Landowner; Country Life; J. of Agricultural and Food Chemistry; J. of Agricultural Economics; Quarterly J. of Forestry; Scottish Forestry; Tropical Agriculture; World Agricultural Economic and Rural Abstracts.*

APPLIED MECHANICS: *Applied Mechanics Review; ASCE Proc. J. of Engineering Mechanics Division; Experimental Mechanics; International J. of Fracture; International J. of Mechanical Sciences; International J. of Solids and Structures; J. of Applied Mechanics; J. of Mechanics and Physics of Solids; J. of Strain Analysis; Mechanism and Machine Theory; Quarterly J. of Mechanics.*

ARCHITECTURE: *Architect's J.; Architectural Assoc. Quarterly; Architectural Design; Architectural Record; Architectural Review; Architectural Science Review; Architectur d'Aujourd'hui; Building Design; Building Science Abstracts; Built Environment; Chartered Surveyor; Design; Landscape Design; RIBA Annual Review of Periodical Articles; RIBA J.; Royal Inst. of Chartered Surveyors—Tech. Info. Serv.*

BANKING: *Bank of England Quarterly Bulletin; Banker; Banker's Magazine; Barclays Bank Review; Federal Reserve Bulletin; Instit. of Bankers J.; Lloyds Bank Review; Midland Bank Review; Moorgate and Wall Street; National Westminster Quarterly Review; Three Banks Review.*

CERAMICS: *American Ceramic Society Bulletin; American Ceramic Society J. with Ceramic Abstracts; British Ceramic Society Trans.*

CHEMISTRY: *Angewandte Chemie; British Ceramic Soc. Trans.; Chemistry and Industry; Chemistry in Britain; Institute of Metal Finishing Transactions; J. of Agricultural and Food Chemistry; J. Of Applied Chemistry and Biotechnology.*

CIVIL ENGINEERING: *ASCE J. of the Eng. Mech. Div.: ASCE J. of the Power Div.; Articles in Civil Engineering; Civil Eng. and Public Works Review; Consulting Engineer; Foundation Facts; Institution of Civil Engineers Proceedings; International Civil Engineering; Pipes and Pipelines International; Quarterly J. of Eng. Geology; Society of Civil Engineering Technicians.*

COMMERCE AND TRADE: *Barclays Review; Bulletin of the European Communities; Business Periodicals Index; Business Archives; Columbia J. of World Business; Financial Times; Harvard Business Review; Industrial Review of Great Britain; J. of Business; Pais Bulletin (incl.) Public Affairs Inf. Service; Research Index; Trade and Industry.*

COMMUNICATION TECHNOLOGY: *Electronics Letters; IEEE Trans. on Antennae and Propagation; IEEE Trans. Broadcast and Television Receivers; IEEE Trans. on Broadcasting; IEEE Trans. on Communications; IEEE Trans. Microwave Theory and Techniques; IEEE Trans. on Vehicular Technology; Independent Broadcasting Title: Technical Review; Pipes and Pipelines International; Post Office Electrical Eng. Journal; Telecommunications; Wireless World.*

COMPONENT TECHNOLOGY: *Building Materials; Electronic Components; IEEE Trans. on Parts, Hybrids and Packaging; Original Equipment Manufacture Design.*

COMPUTING: *Computer Abstracts; Computer and Control Abstracts; Computer and Information Systems; Computer J. Abstracts; Computing Reviews; Accountancy & Data Processing Abstracts (ANBAR); Computer Aided Design; Business Equipment Guide; IBM Technical Disclosure Bulletin; IEEE Trans. on Computers; Computer Education; Computer Survey; Computer Weekly; Computing; Data Processing; Data Processing Practitioner; Data Systems; Datamation; IEEE Computer; ACM (Assoc. for Computer Machinery) Communications; ACM (Assoc. for Computer Machinery J.; Computer J.; Computer Programs in Science and Technology; IBM J. of Research and Development; IBM Systems J.; IEEE Transactions on Computers; International J. of Computer Mathematics; Management Informatics; Software Practice and Experience; Systems—Computers—Controls.*

CONSTRUCTION: *ASCE J. of Construction Division; Building International; Building; Building Design; Building Materials; Building Research; Building Research Establishment Digest; Building Research Establishment News; Building Science; Building Science Abstracts; Building Technology and Management; Building Trades J.; Construction News; Construction Plant and Equipment; Contract J.; Contractors Plant Review; Current Information in the Construction Industry; Department of Environment World; Housing and Construction Statistics; National Builder; New Building Projects; RIBA Annual Review of Periodical Articles; Stone Industries; World Construction.*

CONTROL: *Computer and Control Abstracts; Control & Instrumentation; Control Engineering; Electronics Letters; IEEE Trans. on Automatic Control; IEEE Trans. on Ind. Elect. and Cont. Inst.; IEEE Trans. on Inst. and MEAS; Institution of Electrical Engineers Proc.; International J. of Control; Measurement and Control; Microtechnic; Process Instrumentation; Soviet Automatic Control.*

CORPORATE POLICY: *J. of Business Policy; Long Range Planning.*

EDUCATION: *Audio Visual Communication Review; Audio Visual Language J.; BACIE J.; British Education Index; British J. of Educational Psychology; British J. of Educational Technology; British J. of Guidance and Counselling; Comparative Education; Comprehensive Education; Current Contents: Behavioural, Social and Educational Sciences; Current Index to J. in Education; Education; Education Abstracts; Education and Training; Educational Administration Quarterly; Educational Research; Harvard Educational Review; J. of Curriculum Studies; J. of Educational Administration; J. of Educational Research; J. of Teacher Education; Liberal Education; Programmed Learning; Research in Education; Review of Educational Research; Sociology of Education; Special Education; Teacher; Teachers' World; Times Educational Supplement; Trends in Education; Visual Education.*

ELECTRICAL ENGINEERING: *Electrical and Electronics Abstracts; IEEE Trans. Plasma Science; Light and Lighting; Electrical Reviews; IEEE Trans. on Education; Int. J. of Elect. Eng. Education; CEGB Digest; IEEE Trans. on Antennae and Propagation; IEEE Trans. on Circuit Theory; IEEE Trans. on Electromagnetic Compatibility; IEEE Trans. on Magnetics; IEEE Trans. on Industry Applications; IEEE Trans. on Microwave Theory and Techniques; IEEE Trans. on Parts, Hybrids and Packaging; Industrial Application of Electricity; Inst. of Elect. Eng. Proc.; Inst. of Eng. Australia-Elec. Eng. Trans.*

ELECTRONICS: *Electronic Components; Electronic Engineering; Electronics Letters; IEEE Proceedings; IEEE Trans. on Aerospace and Elect. Syst.; IEEE Trans. on Electron. Devices; IEEE Trans. On Geo. Electronics; IEEE Trans. Indust. Electronics and Control Instrumentation; IEEE Trans. on Parts, Hybrids & Packaging; IEEE Trans. Quantum Electronics; Practical Electronics; Wireless World; Electrical and Electronics Abstracts; IEEE Trans. on Circuit Theory; IEEE Trans. on Solid State Circuits; Microelectronics; Electronic Components; Electronics; IEEE Spectron; IEEE Trans. on Education; Nat. Elect. Rev.; Wireless World.*

ENGINEERING: *Engineering Index Abstracts; Industrial Minerals; Project; Society of Engineers J.; ATOM; BSI News; Engineer; Engineering; Engineering Education; Engineering J. (Canada); Engineering J. (USA); Engineering News Record; Engineering Opportunities; Engineering Outlook; Institution of Eng. of Australia J.; Plant Engineer; Aeronautical J.; IEEE Trans. on Bio-Medical Engineering.*

FINANCE: *Building Societies Gazette; Credit; Engineering Economist; Finance and Development; Financial Statistics; Money Which?; Public Finance Quarterly.*

FOOD SCIENCE: *Food Engineering; Food Manufacture; Food Processing Industry; Food Science and Technology; Food Technology; Institute of Food Science and Technology Proceedings; J. of Agricultural and Food Chemistry; J. of Food Science; J. of Food Science and Technology; J. of Food Technology; Sugar Technology Reviews.*

FUEL TECHNOLOGY: *Building Science Abstracts; Energy Digest; Flambeau; Fuel; Fuel Abstracts and Current Titles; Gas World; Industrial and Process Heating; Institute of Fuel J.; Institute of Gas Engineers J.*

HOTEL and CATERING: *Business Travel World; Caterer and Hotel Keeper; Catering and Hotel Management; Catering Quarterly; Catering Times; Cornell Hotel and Restaurant Administration; Hotel and Restaurant Catering; Hotel Catering and District Management J.; Industrial and Welfare Catering; International Hotel Review.*

INDUSTRIAL DESIGN: *Auto-Style; Computer Aided Design; DISA Information; Design; Design Dialogue; Design Industries; Design Quarterly; Designer; Engineering Designer; Engineering Materials and Design; Industrial Design; Industrial Designers Society of America J.; Machine Design; Mobilia; Original Equipment Manufacture Design.*

INDUSTRIAL RELATIONS: *British J. of Industrial Relations; Columbia J. of World Business; Fortune; Industrial and Labour Relations Review; Industrial Relations; Industrial Relations J.; Industrial Relations Review and Report; Industrial Society; International Labour Review; Wrights Industrial Reports; Supervisory Management; Trades Union News from European Community; Works Management.*

IRON AND STEEL: *British Cast Iron Research Association J.; Iron and Steel Making; Steel Castings Abstracts; Steel Castings Res. and Trade Assoc. J. of Research; Steel Times.*

LAW: *All England Law Reports; Arbitration; Bulletin of European Communities; Cambridge Law J.; Common Market Law Review; Conveyancer and Property Lawyer; Conveyancer and Property Lawyer—Precedents for the Conveyancer; Current Law; Current Law Statutes Annotated; Digest of New Legislation; Halsbury's Law; Halsbury's Statutes; Howard Law J.; International and Comparative Law Quarterly; J. of Business Law; J. of Planning and Environment Law; Justice of the Peace; Knight's Industrial Reports;*

*Law Notes; Law Quarterly Review; Law Society Gazette; Legal Executive; Modern Law Review; New Law J.; Parliamentary Affairs; Property and Compensation Reports; Public Law; Solicitors J.; Weekly Law Reports.*

MANAGEMENT: *Advanced Management J.; American Industrial Hygiene Association J.; Anbar Abstracts; Business Week; Columbia J. of World Business; Communications Management; Data Processing; European Business; Harvard Business Review; Industrial Management; Interfaces; J. of Industrial Economics; J. of Management Studies; J. of Systems Management; Management Abstracts; Management Accounting; Management Decision; Management Education and Development; Management Informatics; Management International Review; Management Review and Digest; Management Science; Management Today; Omega; Research Index; Work Study; Work Study and Management Services; Work Study and O and M Abstracts (Anbar).*

MARKETING: *European J. of Marketing; J. of Marketing; J. of Marketing Research; Market Research Society J.; Market Research Abstracts; Marketing; Marketing and Distribution Abstracts (Anbar); Marketing Forum; Sales Management.*

MATERIALS SCIENCE: *British Foundryman; International J. of Machine Tool Des. and Res.; Metallurgia and Metal Forming; Metals Engineering Quarterly; Modern Casting; Steel Castings Abstracts; Steel Castings Res. and Trade Assoc. J. of Research; International J. of Solids and Structures; J. of Composite Materials; J. of Engineering Materials and Technology: J. of Materials Science; J. of Mechanics and Physics of Solids; J. of Nuclear Materials; Materials Engineering; Materials Science and Engineering; Metallurgist and Materials Technologist; Powder Technology; Refractories J.*

MATHEMATICS: *Mathematical Gazette; Mathematical Reviews; Mathematical Spectrum; Quarterly J. of Mathematics; Royal Society Proceedings A; Association for Computing Machinery J.; Biometrics; Biometrika; Econometrica; Institute of Mathematics and its Applications J.; International J. of Computing Mathematics; International J. of Math. Educat. in Science Bulletin; Mathematics of Computation; Sociometry; Technometrics.*

MECHANICAL ENGINEERING: *British Ship Res. Association J. of Abstracts; Bulletin of Mechanical Engineering Education; Chartered Mechanical Engineer; Institution of Eng. of Australia (Trans.); Institution of Mechanical Eng. Proc.; J. of Engineering for Industry; J. of Mechanical Engineering Science; J. of Sound and Vibration; Machinery; Machines and Tooling; Mechanical Engineering; Mechanical Handling; Mechanism and Machine Theory.*

METALLURGY: *ACTA Metallurgica; British Foundryman; Emen; Institute of Metal Finishing Trans.; Institute of Metals J.; Institute of Mining and Metallurgy. Trans.; International J. of Fracture; International Metallurgical Reviews; J. of Less Common Metals; J. of Metals; J. of Physics C and F; Metal Construction and British Welding J.; Metal Progress; Metal Science J.; Metal Science and Heat Treatment; Metallurgia and Metal Forming; Metallurgical Transactions; Metals Abstracts; Metals and Materials; Metals Engineering Quarterly; Metals Technology; Physics of Metals and Metallography; Powder Metallurgy; Scripta Metallurgia; Sheet Metal Industries.*

MINING: *Canadian Inst. of Mining and Metallurgy; Industrial Minerals; Institution of Mining and Metallurgy Trans.; International J. of Rock Mechanics and Min. Sci.; Mining Engineer.*

OPERATIONAL RESEARCH: *Engineering Economist; Long Range Planning; Management Accounting; Operational Research Quarterly; Operations Research; Production and Inventory Management; Simulation and Games; Socio Economic Planning Sciences; Transportation Research; Transportation Science.*

PERSONNEL MANAGEMENT: *Canadian Personnel and Industrial Relations J.; Industrial Society; Personnel J.; Personnel Management; Personnel Review; Personnel and Training Abstracts (Anbar); Supervisory Management; Works Management.*

PHYSICS: *American J. of Physics; Bibl. on High Temperature Chem. and Physics of Materials; Current Contents—Phys. and Chem. Sci.; Faraday Society—Symposia; Geophysics; IBM J. of Research and Development; IEEE Trans. Plasma Science; IEEE Trans. on Antennae and Propagation; IEEE Trans. on Microwave Theory and Tech.; International J. of Heat and Mass Transfer; Japanese J. of Applied Physics; J. of Applied Physics; J. of Atmospheric and Terrestrial Physics; J. of Chemical Physics; J. of Geophysical Research; J. of Heat Transfer; J. of Mass Spectrometry and Iron Physics; J. of Physics A-F; J. of Scientific Instruments; Heat and Fluid Flow; Philips Research Reports and Supplement; Philosophical Magazine; Physics Education; Physics in Technology; Physical Review A and B; Physics Teacher; Physics Today; Physics Abstracts (Science Abs. Series A); Planetary and Space Science; Royal Society Proceedings.*

POWER ENGINEERING: *ASCE J. of Power Division; CEGB Digest; Energy Digest; IEEE Trans. on Power Apparatus & Systems; Institution of Electrical Eng. Proc.; J. of Eng. for Power; J. of Nuclear Materials; Thermal Engineering; Water Service.*

PRODUCTION ENGINEERING: *CIRP Annals; Engineers Digest; IEEE Trans. Engineering Management; IEEE Trans. Manufacturing Technology; Industrial and Process Heating; Inst. of Metal Finishing Trans.; Int. J. of Production Research; Machinery; Machines and Tooling; Materials Engineering; Materials Performance; Metal Finishing J.; Metal Progress; Metalworking Production; Microtecnic; Production Engineer; Production and Inventory Management; Production Technology; Sheet Metal Industries.*

QUALITY CONTROL: *IEEE Trans. on Reliability; J. of Quality Technology; Quality; Quality Control and Applied Statistics (Abstracts); Quality Engineer; Quality Management and Engineering; Quality Progress.*

SOCIAL WORK: *Abstracts for Social Workers; British J. of Guidance and Counselling; British J. of Social Work; Health and Social Service J.; J. of Research in Crime and Delinquency; Poverty; Social Casework; Social Service Quarterly; Social Trends; Social Work (Today); Social Work (USA).*

STATISTICS: *American Statistical Association J.; Applied Statistics; Biometrics; Biometrika; Econometrica; Oxford Bulletin of Economics and Statistics; Review of Economics and Statistics; Royal St. Soc. J. Series A and B; Statistician; Technometrics.*

STRUCTURAL ENGINEERING: *ASCE J. of Structural Division; American Concrete Inst. J.; Building Research Establishment News; Building Science Abstracts; Ground Engineering; Precast Concrete; Prestressed Concrete Inst. J.; Structural Engineer.*

TAXATION: *Taxation; Taxation Reports; Tax Notes.*

## FOLLOW-UP

We do not suggest that you should regularly read all the journals published in your special area. However, we do suggest that you examine a good number, and then subscribe to one or two.

Reading is itself a definite skill. Activity 37, 'Study Skills', helps you to examine a number of related abilities, and gives some useful references.

# Activity 5
## Facts and assumptions

In life we do not often bother to separate out facts from assumptions. We do not have the time. When I enter my office in the morning I observe facts and make assumptions. I observe that the office door is shut but I assume much more: that the room has been cleaned; that the papers I left on my desk last night are still there; that the furniture is arranged as I left it; and so on. When I go to a meeting, I observe that certain people are present, but I make assumptions: how certain individuals will behave; how long the meeting will last; whether I will be interested or bored; and so on.

Assumptions nearly always outweigh observations and this ability to assume, i.e., to predict, is a valuable human skill, without which progress and behaviour would be painfully slow and limited. However, there are a number of times when I make wrong assumptions: that my office has been cleaned when it hasn't, or that so-and-so will talk all the time and he is silent. Sometimes all this causes is surprise, but sometimes action is based on a false assumption. If I thought so-and-so would attack my ideas at the meeting I might decide attack was the best form of defence and attack him first. When he attacks back my assumption is confirmed. Or is it? Would he have attacked if I had not? This is a self-fulfilling prophecy—when I make an assumption; act on that assumption; and my action causes another to act in a way which confirms my original but false assumption.

Another pitfall is that I may not observe certain facts if I have already made assumptions which are contrary to those facts. If I assume that so-and-so is going to attack me, I only see his aggression and, if I notice friendly acts, interpret them as 'softening-up' tactics. This is 'selective perception'. I see what I want to see; select those things I am looking for. One goes into a room looking for a book and does not notice a new furniture arrangement, because one is not looking for it. There is danger in operating on untested assumptions and perceiving selectively from the environment.

This activity is designed to help build those mental muscles which distinguish 'facts' from 'assumptions'.

## The activity

*Step 1*

Choose a relative stranger who has either recently joined your organization, or whom you have only recently come across.

*Step 2*

Observe him closely and make a list of all those things which you can verify as 'facts': dress, appearance, expressions, behaviour. Philosophically, it is perhaps impossible to justify anything as a fact, but there are some things about which we can be relatively certain. 'He is very tall' (of a 6' 3" man), for instance. But how factual is the statement 'She is very nice'? Even 'very tall' is subjective and may not be regarded as fact when talking about a 6' 3" basketball player. The safest rule is to ask yourself: 'What will I accept as a fact, that is a given or commonly verifiable piece of information, in this particular situation?'

*Step 3*

Now make another list, this time of assumptions. These may be based upon the facts you have observed, but they should be assumptions, guesses, or predictions arising out of those facts on such matters as status, religion, likes or dislikes, personality problems, marital status, habits, opinions, attitudes, and so on.

Some of these assumptions may be relatively safe: it is a fact that he is tall therefore it is fair to assume that 'he finds the office desks uncomfortable to sit at'. Or they might be more 'risky'. 'He is tall', therefore can one assume 'his wife is tall also' or 'he feels embarrassed at being so tall'?

Be honest with yourself and list all the assumptions that come to mind.

*Step 4*

When you have made your list of assumptions, estimate how many will be correct. If possible check these out with him or her, explaining the object of the exercise. Whatever happens you will have made a new acquaintance and possibly a friend!

What proportion of your assumptions were correct?

(If you can't pluck up the courage to approach the person in question, you could ask a friend or colleague to go through the same activity and compare lists. What did you observe that he/she did not? and vice versa? What assumptions did each of you make?)

## FOLLOW-UP

*1. Questions to ponder*

(a)  What did you learn about the nature of 'facts'?

(b) What did you learn about the number of assumptions you habitually make about people and situations?

(c) Did you discover how selective your perception is?

(d) Can you think of other situations at work where you go through similar facts—assumptions, connections?

*2. Further reading*

If you're interested in the questions of perception of others and the problem of discerning what you will accept as 'facts' and what are more clearly 'assumptions', the following two references will be useful: *Social Psychology* by Roger Brown (Collier-Macmillan, 1968). In particular chapter 12 'Impressions of personality, including one's own', pages 610–654. *Social Psychology* by W. W. Lambert and W. E. Lambert (Prentice-Hall, 1964). In particular chapter 3 'Perceiving and judging social events', pages 28–48.

These are only examples of books you might expect to find in your public library. Any general social psychology text should have relevant reading under the heading of 'perception' or 'person perception'.

*3. Further activity*

(a) If you'd like to see how your skills are developing, repeat the activity with the next suitable person, or . . .

(b) Try a variation at the next meeting or interview you attend. Draw up lists of 'facts' and 'assumptions' beforehand or at the very beginning. Observe during the event and check back on your lists afterwards. If you do this once or twice, you might be surprised at (i) how observant you're becoming; (ii) how accurate your assumptions are becoming; (iii) how cautious you are now about making assumptions!

# Activity 6
## Personal journal

LEARNING AREAS: SENSITIVITY TO EVENTS: Analytical skills: Self-knowledge:
Balanced learning habits

An underlying theme running throughout this book is the value of reflecting upon one's own behaviour. If you can do this in a purposeful, insightful manner, you will become more able to tune in to situations and to learn from experiences, and will develop a greater self-awareness and ability to cope with pressures and emotions.

To gain maximum benefit from many of the activities, they should be repeated several times, particularly this one. It is necessary to keep the journal over a period of weeks or even months to get the most out of it.

There is nothing new in the idea of keeping some form of diary. However, to help make such an exercise more meaningful for self-development, this form of personal journal is structured round a simple model of an individual's behaviour in a particular situation.

According to this model, there are three aspects of behaviour:

*1. The individual's FEELINGS*: the way a person behaves is very much determined by his feelings in a given situation. He is often unaware—or at best only half aware—of the nature of his feelings and the effect they are having. In our society there is a tendency to suppress or deny feelings—'the stiff upper lip' is still admired—but if you are to be in control of your behaviour, it is essential to be sensitive to your feelings and their effects.

*2. The individual's THOUGHTS and IDEAS*: in any situation the individual lives through a number of thoughts and ideas. Important among these are the factors he perceives in a situation and ideas about courses of action. These will depend on the various elements of the current situation and will be influenced by the individual's assumptions and the perceptions he brings in from previous experience. Also important will be the new thoughts and ideas that are triggered off by the new situation.

82

*3. The individual's ACTION-TENDENCIES*: The individual will have various action-tendencies: predispositions to certain types of action. For example, in committee and disagreeing strongly with the views of the chairman, he may nonetheless say nothing because he is scared of challenging authority. This fear, or lack of self-confidence, will result in an action-tendency of saying/doing nothing. Another action-tendency could be described as precipitous: a strong need to *do* something rather than to think things out carefully—a tendency which leads to over-hasty action.

Action-tendencies are internal motivations or forces that push individuals towards certain types of action or inaction.

These three elements each influence the individual's action behaviour. Take the example of a manager in committee. The chairman seems to be supporting something with which I, the manager, disagree. My *thoughts/ ideas* are that what he has said is wrong. As a result, my *feelings* are those of concern and excitement. However, due to my *parallel feeling* of fear of ridicule, or fear of challenging authority, my *action-tendency* is to say nothing.

My behaviour in this situation will depend on which of the three elements wins out. Will my ideas and half of my feelings overcome my action-tendency, leading to my making a soundly presented contribution? Or will my other feelings combine with my negative action-tendencies, leading me to remain silent? Or again, perhaps my feelings and action-tendencies will result in my making a fumbling, incoherent statement—i.e., preventing my beautifully logical ideas from getting a just hearing.

The elements depend on each other. For example, my thoughts and ideas about what is being said may well depend on my feelings about the person saying it—and vice versa. We can see that this model of behaviour, although simple, represents a very complicated situation. This can be shown in a diagram (Fig. A6.1), emphasizing the links between thoughts/ideas, feelings, and action-tendencies.

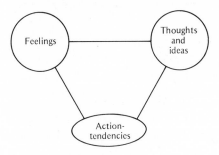

*Figure A6.1*

Feelings, thoughts/ideas, and action-tendencies don't exist in a vacuum. They arise in response to some situational stimulus (in itself affected by previous events). They result in behaviour, which leads to a new situation; and so on.

This is the model around which the 'Personal Journal' is based.

*Figure A6.1*

## The activity

This is carried out over a period of time, and you may find it so useful that it will become established as part of your way of life—something you do all the time. Failing that, you at least will develop a 'mental' personal journal as a permanent way of thinking.

In any case, keep the journal going for a minimum of 20 entries, with at least 4 entries each week. A single entry might cover one specific incident, or may deal with a whole day's activities.

As with physical exercise, it is important to build up performance gradually, and so the activity is presented in three steps of increasing complexity.

*Step 1*

Take an exercise book and mark left and righthand pages as shown in Fig. A6.2.

Obviously this is only a rough guide; if you want more space under any or all of the headings, continue overleaf.

Write, on the lefthand page, a brief description of a happening. This should be factual and objective, and it is useful to include a description of the antecedents and context—i.e., what led up to the situation.

Write down your responses to the situation on the righthand page. Your feelings might have changed during the course of the happening. Identify and note such changes. Look for feelings that were closely followed by different ones. (For example, anger often follows a feeling of being threatened.) Note the thoughts/ideas which came into your mind during the situation; distinguish between facts and assumptions. Then note down your action-

| WHAT HAPPENED | MY RESPONSES |
|---|---|
| | *My feelings* |
| | *My thoughts and ideas* |
| | *My action-tendencies* |
| | *hence* |
| | *My behaviour* |

*Table A6.2*

tendencies. What other factors influenced your action (or non-action). Try to identify ways in which feelings, thoughts, and action-tendencies affect each other. Finally, note down the effect of these elements on your behaviour—what did you actually do? This may have led to another situation, which can form another journal entry.

*Step 2*

After seven or eight entries, move on to the second phase. Complete the exercise as in Step 1, but then go on to evaluate your behaviour by recording under a new heading 'Self-Evaluation', how you feel about your feelings, thoughts/ideas, action-tendencies, and behaviour. Do you feel good, bad, happy, sad, adequate, inadequate, guilty, disappointed, frustrated, etc.? Try to explore these self-evaluations—what do they tell you about yourself?

*Step 3*

After seven or eight entries at Step 2, take the journal further by adding, in the next series, another heading—'Learning'. Record what you feel you have learned from the 'happenings'—from your feelings, thoughts/ideas, action-tendencies, behaviour, and self-evaluation.

Look back over previous journal entries, to see if patterns emerge that tell you something of significance about yourself, other people, situations, and so on.

Now write the words NOW WHAT? And try the hardest part of all. Set yourself concrete goals for behaviour that will use in a significant way the new insights and learning that you have derived from the whole exercise.

FOLLOW-UP

By compiling the journal over a period of time you should become more insightful about situations and your behaviour in them, and you will learn how to learn from everyday experience.

# Activity 7
## Decision making

An important aspect of the manager's job concerns the making of decisions. Robert Townsend[1] commented that something like 40 per cent of the decisions he made while Managing Director of Avis turned out to be wrong in some way. Most important, though, he made them. Given Townsend's proven ability, this puts your and my batting averages on correct decision making into perspective. It looks as though first-class managers average 50–60 percent correct decisions. (It takes a first-class manager to admit this.) Most of us have a remarkable facility for justifying our actions or for 'rationalizing'. We do this even when not called to account by superiors; we justify ourselves to ourselves. If we did less of this we would recognize how many of our decisions turned out to be wrong, sometimes initial decisions which created a dozen crisis/decision points. A manager's decision to authorize a new project will spawn dozens more as it gets underway— intermediate outcomes calling for intermediate decisions and so on.

All decisions are hedged about with uncertainty—otherwise there would be no decision to make—some being more uncertain than others.

Broadly speaking there are two ways of making decisions:

Following a 'rational' process of planning: specifying alternatives, criteria, and pay-off probabilities until the 'correct' solution emerges.

Following 'hunches' or intuition: taking action without planning, because action creates information and information reduces uncertainty.

Depending on training and personality most of us use one of these modes more than the other—even to the exclusion of the other. This is perhaps natural, but it limits our capacity for meeting different kinds of decisions. Complex decisions may demand the use of both modes at different times.

**Activity**

Below are some sample decisions. Although some may be complex we'll treat them as simple and say that one mode of decision making is more suitable than the other.

*Step 1*

Read each sample decision and decide whether it is 'rational' (Type A) or 'intuitive' (Type B).

1. Getting yourself from your place of work to a meeting in another specific location.

2. Being dropped anywhere in the country, without knowing where, with £1, and the task of getting home. Imagine yourself standing in open country surrounded by a light fog.

3. Choosing the means of communicating some minor redundancies in the company, given a 48-hour deadline and a partly unionized labour force.

4. Selecting a bonus payment scheme for a work section where workloads are extremely variable and where payment has previously been on a flat hourly rate.

5. Deciding how to approach your boss about a favour you want from him and knowing that he can be very moody and changeable.

6. Deciding how to run a particular appraisal interview.

You might well say that you would use both decision types as appropriate. We say that in *broad terms* the decisions split down like this:

| Decision | Type |
|----------|------|
| 1 | A |
| 2 | B |
| 3 | A |
| 4 | A |
| 5 | B |
| 6 | B |

*Table A7.1*    A = rational; B = intuitive.

*Step 2*

The choice of decision type has a very marked effect on how you behave when faced with a particular problem. Try thinking aloud about a couple of the decisions in the list above.

Jot down on a piece of paper the steps you would take to make the decisions set out as 1 and 2.

Then answer the following:

(a) Are your notes very similar for decisions 1 and 2, or very different?

(b) Which did you find easier: 1 or 2?

You probably found decision 1 easier to tackle.

Decision 1 is 'rational'; the goal is clear and there are relatively well-structured alternatives. In the jargon—there is a specific goal with limited goal paths. Therefore, a rational decision is possible by sifting the alternatives against the criteria and choosing appropriately. We can spell out this rational process using decision 1 as an example:

| *Problem solving stages* | *Decision 1* |
|---|---|
| 1. Analyse the problem in terms of:<br>(a) How things are.<br>(b) How I want things to be. | 1. I am at work and I want to get to the meeting in London. |
| 2. Specify *your objective* in terms of the change you want to bring about, i.e., A → B. | 2. (Already stated in 1 above.) |
| 3. Specify the alternative courses of action open to you to achieve the objective. | 3. Go by:  — car<br>— train<br>— taxi<br>— bus<br>— aeroplane<br>— get a lift from a colleague |
| 4. Specify the *criteria*, i.e., what characteristics must a course of action have to achieve your objective. | —I need to be there by 10 a.m. and I don't want to stay overnight (before or after).<br>—It must not cost more than £20.<br>—It would be useful to be able to read the papers for the meeting on the journey.<br>—I need to be fresh on arrival. |
| 5. Choose the alternative which best meets the criteria. | 5. The train meets all criteria. The car fails on criteria three and four, the taxi on criterion two; the bus is noisy and fails on four; there is no 'plane until 10 a.m. and this fails on criterion one; travelling with a colleague is possible but would hinder criterion three. |
| 6. Implement the alternative. | 6. Catch the train. |
| 7. Check whether you have achieved your goal, and if not, return to 1. | 7. Did you get to the meeting on time and fresh? |

*Table A 7.2*

Decision 2 does not lend itself to such an analysis. There is a clear goal: you want to get home; but you have no idea where you are and there are no clearly structured alternative actions open to you. There is much more uncertainty in this situation than in decision 1. With this lack of information there is a limit to the amount of planning you can do before taking action.

In well-structured situations *planning* can usefully precede *action*. In unstructured situations, where uncertainty predominates, it is better to get into action quickly because *action generates information.* In decision 2, an intelligent action is to walk in a fixed direction (not in a circle) because this would give you maximum chance of uncovering information: a stream; a path; a road; a clearing in the mist, etc. If you find a path then you clearly have a much more structured choice—whether to follow it and, if so, in which direction. As paths always lead from one place to another, you will tend to follow it in the hope of finding out where you are, i.e., to generate more information. Eventually, you will generate enough information to know what kind of a problem you have in getting home, and what the alternatives are. You are then back in a decision 1-type 'rational' process.

In conditions of uncertainty, *action has to proceed planning*, because action generates the information required for planning. Or to put it another way, the first objective in uncertain situations is to generate information. You choose an action to this end and pursue it until further information is obtained at which point planning may be appropriate.

In decision 5 there are no obvious alternative courses of action because the boss is *unpredictable.* A carefully planned strategy could be disastrous—a plan possesses a momentum which is hard to modify. The best approach would be to keep on neutral ground until his behaviour provides a clue to his mood, after which you can plan what action to take.

Decision 6 is a similar situation unless you regard it as a one-way process—in which case you can adopt a 'rational' approach without the need to generate information about the other person's feelings and views. Most interpersonal situations demand the *action before planning* approach. This is the area of decision making which creates many problems for managers. Those who are able to suspend their planning skills to generate sufficient information about alternatives and criteria *according to other people* will usually make better decisions. They are more 'socially skilled' than managers who impose a previously-planned 'rational' decision upon others.

To summarize: use the 'rational' process for well-structured situations; use an *action before planning* approach to situations where there is little or no information (you have first to be able to admit/recognize that there is little or no information).

The following advice is useful in uncertain situations:

—Regard obtaining information as an objective in itself.

—Be prepared to get quickly into action of a kind which will generate information
—Be prepared to go through many cycles of action → information → planning → action.

All this can be fitted into the 'rational' decision-making process if you recognize its cyclical nature; the need to start with information-getting as the objective; the need to move into action on an experimental basis.

*Step 3*

If you think you understand the difference between the two approaches to decision making, this step will test you further.

Reflect upon a recent or current decision and ask yourself:

—Has 'information-getting' been an objective?
—Has there been enough experimental action?
—Have I picked up all the information available from experimental action and from elsewhere?
—Have I analysed the available information carefully and did it result in improved understanding?

FOLLOW-UP

There are a number of well-known available courses and books on problem solving/decision making. One of the best-known techniques is a 'rational' one, Kepner-Tregoe, described in a book *The Rational Manager* by C. H. Kepner and B. B. Tregoe (McGraw-Hill, 1965). A rather more technical text is *The Anatomy of Decisions* by P. G. Moore and H. Thomas (Penguin, Modern Management, 1976). A pleasing aspect of the latter is the inclusion of exercises (with answers at the back) attached to each chapter.

REFERENCE

1. Townsend, R., *Up the Organization*, Coronet Books, 1971.

# Activity 8
## Planning and decision-making techniques

LEARNING AREAS: ANALYTICAL SKILLS: Professional knowledge

Numerous planning and decision-making techniques, each with many variations, are available to managers. Opinions vary about the usefulness of such techniques, a common criticism being that techniques work well on classroom type problems specially designed to show how they work, but that problems that managers actually experience rarely fit neatly with the techniques.

However, there are a number of basic techniques (with variations) which any manager could usefully know about. From the point of view of self-development in the area of decision-making and planning techniques, there are plenty of resources available, with books, manuals, and courses on all of them. Most large organizations will have specialists from whom advice could be sought.

Here we provide you with an exercise to check and extend your awareness of some current techniques. If any of them seem pertinent to your problem and worth going into further, you should look for further reading, courses, or help by experts.

There are two points to make about management techniques which stem from the fact that various individuals have *specialized* in each of the techniques and devoted much work to them. They have developed variations and refinements of each of the basic techniques, and entered into complex debate with each other about various points of application. They have, understandably, been most interested in complex and ambitious applications of these techniques, often involving project teams working on a single problem over many months, sometimes making extensive use of computers. Against this background we make two claims that you might like to consider (particular experts might disagree with us!):

1. that the *core idea* in each technique is relatively simple (as are most good ideas) and easily grasped by a normal, intelligent person;

2. application of the techniques can be brief. A simple useful application of most of the techniques can be carried out in 15 minutes on the back of

an envelope. Indeed, once the idea of each technique has been grasped, it should be possible to incorporate some of the key ideas and principles into your thinking, and thus apply the techniques 'inside your head'. The main payoff from studying management techniques may be from the general effect this has on how you think, rather than through formal and explicit application of the techniques.

**Activity**

*Step 1*

Look at the list of techniques/methods below, and ask yourself if they mean anything to you. Write under each what you know about them.

Critical path analysis/network planning.

Value analysis.

Linear programming.

Break-even-point analysis.

Cost-benefit analysis.

Cost-effectiveness analysis.

Discounted cash flow.

*Step 2*

Compare your understanding with the brief descriptions below:

*Critical path analysis/network planning.* A method of planning for complex, often one-off, projects like putting up a building, installing a new plant, moving an operation from one location to another. In such operations a whole series of tasks have to be done in the right order at the right time for an overall objective to be achieved on time.

The overall method is to list the tasks to be done, work out the order of priorities, draw a 'map' of operations something like Fig. A8.1 (though, of course, much more complicated). The idea is that to do the overall job one has to work down all the 'paths' from left to right.

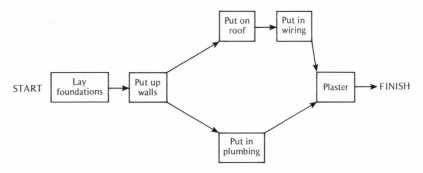

*Figure A8.1*

From here it is possible to plan time and resources for each task, work out which sequence of operations, if delayed, would delay the whole project (this sequence is the 'critical path').

*Value analysis.* This is a process of taking something that is produced, at a cost, to perform a function (usually a product, but it can be a service) and analysing what the cost goes on (parts, assembly tasks, etc.), assessing what these cost elements actually contribute to the performance of the product's function. On the basis of this, ways of cheapening the product without impairing its ability to perform its function can be sought.

*Linear programming.* The linear programming problem is exemplified by the farmer who has available a choice of feedstuff for his cattle, each at different prices, each with different proportions of, say, protein, fat, and carbo-hydrate in them. He knows what his cattle require, in terms of minimum quantities of the three forms of food. His problem is to work out the cheapest combination of the available foodstuffs to meet these requirements.

*Break-even-point analysis.* What it costs to make most mass produced goods can be split more or less into 'fixed' and 'variable' costs. Fixed costs are those which are incurred once you have decided to set up facilities for production.

Variable costs are those that increase in proportion to the number of items you make. In car manufacture, setting up a production line is a fixed cost, the materials and labour that go into making the cars is a variable cost, because for each extra car you produce the more you need of them. The cost of producing various numbers of products can therefore be shown on a graph like that of Fig. A8.2.

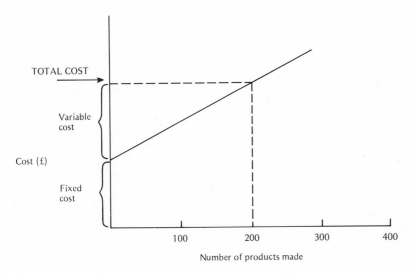

*Figure A8.2*

Another graph can be drawn (Fig. A8.3) relating revenue to number of products sold:

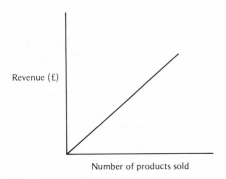

*Figure A8.3*

The slope of the line is determined by the price. The two graphs can be put on top of each other (Fig. A8.4).

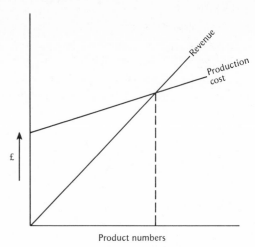

Figure A8.4

The break-even point is where the two lines meet. At this point revenue from sales = production cost and you have 'broken even'. Make and sell more than that and you have a financial return. Make and sell less and you are making a loss.

This kind of analysis is particularly relevant to pricing decisions, and deciding whether it is worth going into a certain line of business.

*Cost-benefit analysis.* This is simply looking at decision 5 in terms of what it would *cost* to go for each alternative, and what the benefit would be from pursuing each alternative, in cost terms. Thus, for example, a transport firm might evaluate different makes and sizes of lorries for its fleet in terms of purchase cost, maintenance costs, and running costs against the return they would get over the lorries' life.

*Cost-effectiveness analysis.* Cost-effectiveness analysis is intended for situations where it is difficult to quantify the benefit side of the equation. It starts from the point of assuming that one wants to do something, looks for alternatives that are equally effective in doing it, and chooses the cheapest.

Thus, for example, a firm may decide that it must provide its employees with a canteen providing a given level of service at given hours, and at a given meal price. It then looks at alternative ways of doing this, for example hiring a catering contractor or taking on staff, works out what the alternatives cost, and makes a choice.

*Discounted cash flow.* Many business decisions involve choosing a line of action that entails making expenditures at different points of time in the future, in the hope of generating revenue at other points of time in the future. Thus, in going into the transport business there is the initial cost of vehicles, and the further costs of maintenance, fuel, and driver's wages spread over the life of the vehicles, plus expenditure on replacing mechanical parts, etc. Coming in should be a steady flow of revenue from freight charges paid by customers. A decision like this involves working out if one would end up better off by going in for this enterprise, and better off by enough to make it worth the trouble.

Because £100 now is not worth the same as the promise of £100 in one year's time, it is not enough to calculate expected cash flow out (costs) and in (revenue). Discounted cash flow is allowing for this by correcting expected costs and revenues at different times to their value at the same time (usually now). This is done by assuming a discount rate (which might be the interest rate at which money can be borrowed, or an estimate of inflation, or a rate fixed by the organization for the purpose) and using this to 'correct' the value of revenues and costs.

If a rate of 20 per cent is assumed (as an estimate of likely inflation, or because this is the cost of borrowing money to finance the project), the £100 would be worth £120 in one year's time, and therefore £100 in one year's time is worth

$$£\frac{100 \times 100}{120} = £83\tfrac{1}{3} \text{ now.}$$

Cost or revenue of £100 in one year's time would be counted as £83$\tfrac{1}{3}$ now. Thus all costs and revenues of a project can be corrected to current value equivalents to get a more accurate estimate of the value of the project.

FOLLOW-UP

1. Think carefully whether any of these techniques 'fit' any of your problems.

2. 'Do it yourself' on a specific problem, working out the way from the descriptions above.

3. Choose the techniques that interest you and follow them up with further reading and study.

# Activity 9
## Choosing solutions with a chance

LEARNING AREAS: ANALYTICAL SKILLS: Proactivity: Social skills

One of the criticisms levelled at 'rational problem solving' is that it is easier to decide what needs to be done than to make it happen—to implement the decision. The logical thing is to take 'implementability' into account when choosing solutions; you must be able to put them into practice.

Here are three checklists or 'implementability' criteria, taken from consultants' folklore (consultants have big implementation problems since they rarely have access to formal authority to enforce solutions):

(From Alec Roger):
For a solution to be acceptable it must be seen as:

—technically feasible (it must look as though it will actually work);

—politically acceptable (will not involve changes seen as against the interests of anyone powerful enough to stop it);

—administratively convenient (consistent with the customs, procedures and practices of the organization, so that it is feasible for the people who actually have to do the work).

(From Tom Lupton):
For a solution to be worth attempting there needs to be conviction by all concerned:

—that it will work (technically feasible as above);

—that 'they' will work it ('they' is everybody whose cooperation is needed to put it into practice);

—that it will pay (in money or whatever terms are seen as important).

(From Don Binsted):

For a recommended course of action to be accepted:

—it must be seen as relevant to some problem that really is bothering the people who have to accept or reject it;

—it must suggest clearly a state of affairs that would be generally accepted as better;

—it must offer at least a first and useful step towards a better state of affairs, which is easy for the people concerned to take.

**Activity**

Choose a problem you are having in getting something done, or in getting an idea, solution, or proposal accepted.

Now draw up a list, as in Table A9.1, of the people involved, concerned, or affected by your idea. Write their names in the lefthand column. These are the people to whom you must 'sell' your proposal.

In the middle column, note the 'implementability' criteria that each of these people will require if they are to accept your proposal. As a guideline you can use the sets of criteria given above, but you will probably be able to identify other criteria specific to particular individuals or groups.

| Other parties concerned | Criteria by which other parties will be judging the idea | Match/Mismatch between criteria and proposal |
|---|---|---|
|  |  |  |

*Table A9.1*

If you cannot identify appropriate criteria in some cases—discuss it with the people involved. It is also a good idea, when you think you know the criteria that the various people are looking for, to check out your perception with them. It is surprising how often we make false assumptions about other people—their needs, motives, and interests.

Having identified and checked the criteria that involved/affected parties will use to judge your suggestion, use the final column to note the way in which your idea meets, or fails to meet, each criterion.

When you have done this, you will have a much clearer idea of the likelihood of your plan gaining acceptance, and you will have identified changes you may need to make to have a better chance of acceptance.

## FOLLOW-UP

This activity should be incorporated into your on-going managerial life. By being sensitive to the interests of other people, and bearing these in mind when proposing changes, you will have a much greater chance of getting changes accepted and of being an effective member of a management team.

# Activity 10
## Role set analysis

The concept of 'role' has come to have a central place in management theories. Decision-making roles, leadership roles, supervisory roles are a few examples of the frequent use we make of this term.

The term 'role' is borrowed from the stage where an actor may perform in the role of soldier, king, or lover. In this sense, it is an act or a series of actions. In life we perform many roles—as husband/wife; father/mother; neighbour; son/daughter. Although we remain ourselves—as does the actor passing from role to role—our behaviour is largely determined by the role we are occupying at a given time. Indeed, if we don't alter behaviour to fit into the appropriate role we run into trouble—as you will if you speak to your spouse on the 'phone at work as though he/she were a junior working colleague. Errors of this sort—which we sometimes make—are the results of 'role' conflict.

Role conflict occurs because all roles make demands on our behaviour. Attached to each role are the other people—'significant others'—who make up the role network. These people all have expectations about the way in which the person occupying the role should behave. For example, as a manager, my boss expects me to motivate and control my subordinates; my subordinates expect me to help them and provide them with the means to do their work; my fellow managers expect me to cooperate and liaise with them on jobs which affect us both.

Role conflict occurs in a number of ways:

- —Because two people make opposing or conflicting demands on the role-holder, e.g., the boss who wants the manager to discipline his people while the subordinates want protection from the boss.

- —Because we fill many different roles in quick succession and the demands of one role may conflict with the demands of another, e.g., my role as a manager conflicts with my role as husband and father when I need to work late or at the weekend.

—Because roles carry expectations for behaviour which we personally do not find congenial, e.g., in my role as a manager I have to overlook certain commercial practices, such as giving 'gifts' to clients, which I disapprove of from an ethical viewpoint.

Role conflict is one of the major causes of managerial stress—to avoid stress, role relationships have to be managed like any other part of the job. Role is also an important concept because all our social behaviour is conducted in roles—our actual 'selves' or 'personalities' can never be directly observed.

The value of studying your role as a manager is that:

—You clarify your position within your organization.

—You establish what demands and expectations are made on you in your role.

—You identify possible and actual areas of conflict which helps to reduce the stress.

—You lay the foundations for improving your role performance and hence your general ability as a manager.

## Activity

This activity is designed to achieve the four goals outlined above. All you need is a pen and some paper.

### Step 1

Take a large sheet of paper and draw a circle in the middle to represent the role you occupy at work. Label this circle, e.g., 'Office Manager' (John Brown). Now draw in around the periphery smaller circles to represent all the 'significant others' in the role network of the office manager. These are all the people who make demands upon and have expectations about the role. In addition, the role has reciprocal expectations and makes demands upon them.

You can show the strength of a particular link by making that 'significant other' nearer the centre. Those people with whom you have daily contact probably make more demands and have more expectations of you than those you meet weekly. The role network for the office manager might look like Fig. A10.1:

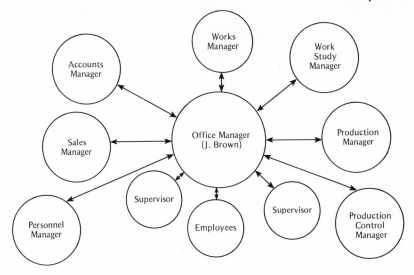

*Figure A10.1*

*Step 2*

When you have completed your role network it is a useful idea to ask someone else what they think about it.

Have you included all significant role relationships?

How different is your role network from others around you?

How does it feel to be the 'man-in-the-middle' serving all these masters?

*Step 3*

If you are satisfied that you have included all the vital role relationships in your job, take another sheet of paper and make a chart. Put down on the lefthand side of the page all the roles which make demands upon your role. Put across the top three columns: 'Their demands/expectations of me'; 'My expectations and demands of them'; 'Possible conflict areas'.

The office manager's chart might look like Table A10.1:

| Role | Their demands/ expectations of me | My expectations/ demands of them | Possible conflict areas? |
|------|-----------------------------------|----------------------------------|--------------------------|
| Supervisors (2) | 1. Fair allocation of work | 1. Achieve set work targets | |
| | 2. Support for their actions | 2. Deal with most grievances and 'man-management' problems | Supervisor actions especially on discipline and grievances are not always consistent with company per- sonnel policy |
| | 3. Personal support e.g., to listen and be available | 3. Keep me informed about a variety of things, e.g., current work loads; supply of materials; personnel issues etc. | |
| | 4. To provide resources to allow them to get the work done | | |
| | 5. Set realistic work targets | 4. Be proactive— set own work targets in consultation with me | Supervisors dependent on me—will not take responsi- bility. |
| Employees (16) | 1. To treat them fairly | 1. To work well and achieve work targets | |
| | 2. To arbitrate over matters of disagreement with supervisors | | Cannot satisfy both employees' demands on me to arbitrate *and* supervisors' demands for support of their actions |
| AND SO ON . . . | | | |

*Table A10.1*

*Step 4*

There are a number of ways in which this role chart may help.

First, do you know what are all the demands and expectations of you? Are you sure you have them all right. It is not unknown for managers confronted with this question to fail even with their boss!

Obviously if you don't know—check it out.

Second, does your perception of their expectations/demands of you fit with theirs? If you asked them would they agree with what you'd written?

The obvious way to check this is to ask them—if you can.

Last, what conflicts appear—between you and your role demands—between different expectations etc.?

How can you resolve or cope with these?

Sometimes the answer is fairly simple. For example, on the office manager's role chart (Table A10.1), the first conflict area—'Supervisor actions especially on discipline and grievances are not always consistent with personnel policy'—perhaps points to a training need.

FOLLOW-UP

If the concept of role interests you, *Roles and Relationships* by Ralph Ruddock (Routledge and Kegan Paul, 1969) makes good reading. On the way in which roles can be defined, changed, and negotiated for organization effectiveness, Roger Harrison's article 'When power conflicts trigger team spirit', *European Business*, Spring, 1972 is a brilliant illustration of how sociological concepts can be turned into managerial aids. His concept of 'role negotiation' is becoming increasingly used in organizations.

# Activity 11
## Planning change

This activity consists of a planning tool designed to help you analyse events and problems from an action point of view. The tool is developed from a systems approach to problems and the basic idea is generally credited to Kurt Lewin whose 'field theory' described a field of forces or pressures acting on any particular event at any particular time.[1] All situations can be seen as being in temporary equilibrium, i.e., the forces acting to change the situation are balanced by the forces acting to resist the change.

We can depict this with a simple diagram:

Figure A11.1

Being able to accept this view of social situations may be something of a problem itself. This view of events is a dynamic one, which sees temporariness in all things and requires a somewhat existential standpoint. What it does offer to the manager is the opportunity of seeing situations as being potentially changeable—if he can identify the forces and seek to change their direction or strength.

Use this activity for a problem that has been worrying you and which seems intractable. The Force Field Analysis will make the options clearer and bring a vague problem into focus and be more 'do-able'.

### Activity

This invites you to carry out a Force Field Analysis of a particular problem which is facing you at present. It proceeds in a number of stages which include a worked example with which to compare yours.

106

Choose a problem and write it down.

It must be a real one which concerns you right now. The example taken here is that of a manager concerned about the rapid rise of accidents in his section.

Define the problem in specific terms.

Who is involved?

What is the magnitude of the problem?

What other factors bear on the situation?

E.g., accidents have risen in Department B over the last six months. Days lost per month through accidents were averaging $5\frac{1}{2}$ per cent at that time; they have now risen to 10 per cent. Relevant factors may include a recent influx of new operatives and a change in bonus system to encourage greater output.

Now state specifically how you would like to influence or change the situation. Try to make this as measurable as possible, so that you can set a clear target and know when you are reaching it. Sometimes this may not be possible, but try.

E.g., 'I would like to reduce the days lost per month through accidents to, say, five or six per cent.'

Looking at the problem as a temporary equilibrium held in place (for the moment) by pushing and restraining forces, list these forces operating on your problem.

(a) What are the forces which would move the present situation towards my goal? (PUSHING FORCES)

 (i)

 (ii)

 (iii)

 (iv)

 (v)

 (vi)

(b) What are the forces resisting or stopping the situation approaching my goal? (RESTRAINING FORCES)

(i)

(ii)

(iii)

(iv)

(v)

(vi)

For example, on the problem of reducing Department B's accident rate:

(a)  PUSHING FORCES (to reduce accident rate):

(i) Manager's desire to lower the rate;
(ii) Company's concern at its image;
(iii) Employee's concern at injuries and costs incurred;
(iv) Union concern at injuries and costs incurred;
(v) Planned safety training courses for union representatives.

(b)  RESTRAINING FORCES  (tending to increase accident rate):

(i) Influx of new operators trained under government 'crash-course' scheme;
(ii) Company's need for increased output;
(iii) New individual bonus to increase output;
(iv) Casual attitude of younger employees concerning general behaviour and use of safety equipment;
(v) Resentment of some older employees at being pushed on output;
(vi) Attitude of older employees to safety regulations.

Make sure you have listed all the forces operating on the problem. Have you included:

—the motivations of individuals and groups involved?

—organizational policies and procedures?

—outside forces operating in the work environment?

When all the forces are listed, rank them as being of,

HIGH ⎫
MEDIUM ⎬ POWER
LOW ⎭

Do this for both PUSHING and RESTRAINING FORCES.

*Step 6*

Now diagram the forces using the length of the arrows to indicate the magnitude of the force. In the example in Fig. A11.2 the Manager's desire to reduce the rate is a HIGH power PUSHING force, while the casual attitude of younger employees is a MEDIUM power RESTRAINING force.

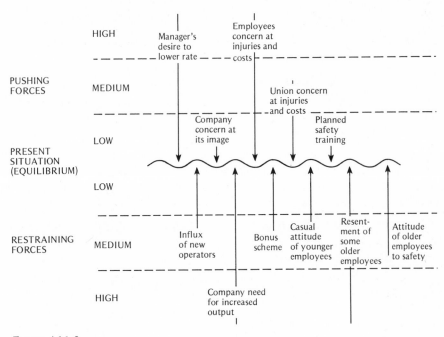

*Figure A11.2*

*Step 7*

Now prepare a strategy for changing the situation.

Remember:

(a) *That if you increase PUSHING forces you often create greater resistance in people and in systems.*

(b) *Change is most easily accepted when it requires a minimum of effort and disruption.*

Can you:

(a) Maintain PUSHING forces, but reduce any of the RESTRAINING forces?

(b) Find new PUSHING forces?

(c) If you must PUSH more, choose forces which do not increase resistance?

(d) Divert any RESTRAINING forces to new targets or in new directions?

(e) Are you sure that it is not one of your PUSHING forces which created the problem in the first place? Would a reduction in this PUSH also reduce the RESTRAINING force?

Your strategy should include the following steps:

(a) The stages to occur in sequence, with rough timings. Activity 8— 'Planning and Decision-Making Techniques' may help here.

(b) The resources you will need at each stage, particularly people who can help.

(c) Sub-goals to evaluate against in checking your progress. (A single far-off goal is somewhat daunting in its unattainability and difficult to plan against.)

## FOLLOW-UP

As an analysis tool, Force Field Analysis can be used to examine any problem situation. More than just a technique, it is a way of seeing situations as being only in temporary equilibrium and amenable to change.

Some references to readings on change have been given in other follow-up sections (see particularly Activity 17). An excellent, although somewhat academic book, devoted entirely to readings on planned change is *The Planning of Change* edited by W. G. Bennis, K. D. Benne and R. Chin (Holt, Rinehart and Winston, 2nd edn., 1970).

## REFERENCES

1. Lewin, K., *Field Theory in Social Science*, Harper, 1951.

# Activity 12
## Analysis of experiences

LEARNING AREAS: ANALYTICAL SKILLS: Balanced learning habits:
Self-knowledge: Sensitivity to events

The successful manager is able to sense what is happening in work situations; he is aware of the elements and factors involved, and of the way in which these factors are complexly related. Furthermore, he can recognize the effects of these factors on his own behaviour and, conversely, the effects of his behaviour on these factors. He is able to use this awareness and sensitivity to learn from everyday experiences.

One relatively long-term method of developing these abilities is through continued use of a 'Personal Journal' (Activity 6). However, there are times when a more detailed analysis is useful, and for these this particular activity can be recommended.

To save you checking back, we set out again here the same model of an individual's behaviour in a situation.

1. *The individual's FEELINGS:* the way a person behaves is very much determined by his feelings in a given situation. He is often unaware—or at best only part aware—of the nature of his feelings and the effect they are having. In our society there is a tendency to suppress or deny feelings—'the stiff upper lip' is still much admired—but if you are to be in control of your behaviour, it is essential to be sensitive to your feelings and their effects.

2. *The individual's THOUGHTS AND IDEAS:* in any situation the individual lives through a number of thoughts and ideas. Important among these are the factors he perceives in a situation and ideas about courses of action. These will depend on the various elements in the current situation and will be influenced by the individual's assumptions and the perceptions he brings in from previous experiences. Also important will be the new thoughts and ideas triggered off by the new situation.

3. *The individual's ACTION-TENDENCIES:* The individual will have various action-tendencies: predispositions to certain types of action. For example, in committee and disagreeing strongly with the chairman, he may nonetheless say nothing because he is scared of challenging authority. This fear or lack of self-confidence will result in an action-tendency of saying/doing nothing.

111

Another action-tendency could be described as precipitous: a strong need to *do* something rather than think things out carefully—a tendency which leads to over-hasty action.

Action-tendencies are internal motivations or forces that push individuals towards certain types of action or inaction.

These three elements each influence the individual's behaviour. Take the example of a manager in committee. The chairman seems to be supporting something with which I, the manager, disagree. My thoughts/ideas are that what he has said are wrong. As a result my *feelings* are those of concern or excitement. However, due to my parallel feeling of fear of ridicule, or fear of challenging authority, my *action-tendency* is to say nothing.

My behaviour in this situation will depend upon which of the three elements wins out. Will my ideas and half my feelings overcome my action-tendency, leading to my making a soundly presented contribution? Or will my other feelings combine with my negative action-tendencies, leading me to remain silent? Or again, perhaps my feelings and action-tendencies will result in my making a fumbling, incoherent statement—i.e., preventing my beautifully logical ideas from getting a fair hearing.

The elements depend on each other. For example, my thoughts and ideas about what is being said may well depend upon my feelings about the person saying it—and vice versa. We can see that this model of behaviour, although simple, represents a very complicated situation. This can be shown as in Fig. A12.1, emphasizing the links between thoughts/ideas, feelings, and action-tendencies.

*Figure A12.1*

Feelings, thoughts/ideas, and action-tendencies don't exist in a vacuum. They arise in response to some situational stimulus (in itself affected by previous events). They result in behaviour, which leads to a new situation; and so on.

*Figure A12.2*

To develop skill in using this activity, you are recommended to approach it in two steps. The first looks at some past events and analyses them. When you have got used to doing this, you then move on to the second step and analyse current events—situations that are still on-going and not yet resolved.

*Step 1*

Choose a recent significant event or situation. 'Significant' means something challenging, worrying, or difficult. Choose a situation that you consider you handled well—or one which you regard as a failure.

Identify the individuals who, in addition to yourself, were involved.

Cast your mind back to the circumstances leading up to the event. Try to recall your feelings, thoughts/ideas, action-tendencies, and behaviour. Note these down, using Table A12.1 as a framework.

Now try to identify the feelings, thoughts/ideas, action-tendencies, and behaviour of each of the other persons who were significantly involved. This will be difficult; we can seldom say that we *know* how someone else is feeling. What we do is estimate or assume and you need to do that here.

If you have difficulty filling out this part of the table, the best source of information is the people themselves.

Check out with them how they were feeling, thinking, acting, behaving. You will always find it instructive to check the validity of your judgement by checking with the people involved.

At this stage think about the significance of the feelings that you **were** unable to identify, or that you assumed incorrectly.

Are you better at estimating feelings, or ideas, or action-tendencies?

Are there some people whose reactions you can perceive accurately, and others you cannot?

Now move on. Note down your perceptions of your own and others' responses *during* the event. Again, check with other people if necessary. Next note down the responses *after* the event.

| People involved | Responses | Before the event | During the event | After the event |
|---|---|---|---|---|
| Me | My feelings | | | |
| | My thoughts/ideas | | | |
| | My action-tendencies | | | |
| | My actual behaviour | | | |
| Other 1 | His feelings | | | |
| | His thoughts/ideas | | | |
| | His action-tendencies | | | |
| | His actual behaviour | | | |
| Other 2 | His feelings | | | |
| | His thoughts/ideas | | | |
| | His action-tendencies | | | |
| | His actual behaviour | | | |
| etc. | etc. | | | |

*Table A12.1*

Study your tabled notes and answer the following:

(a) In what ways were responses related to each other? What caused what?

(b) How do you feel about the way you handled the situation? What, if anything, could you have done differently? What do you think the consequences would have been?

(c) What do you learn from this?

*Step 2*

When you have practised this method of situational analysis over four or five past, significant events, apply it to a current situation—something of significance with which you are now involved.

(a) Analyse the situation so far. Check out your perceptions of other people's responses.

(b) So far, how are the various responses involved?

(c)  How do you feel about the way the situation is shaping up so far? What are you going to do? What do you think the consequences will be?

(d)  Do what you have decided to do.

(e)  Continue with the analysis. Are the effects as predicted?

(f)  Repeat steps (c)–(e) until you think the event is over.

(g)  What have you learned from this event? What are the implications of this learning for your future actions?

FOLLOW-UP

This way of looking at situations should become part of your everyday managerial life. You should start considering situations in terms of the perceptions and responses of the other people involved—checking these out to make sure that you are not basing your actions on invalid assumptions.

# Activity 13
## Catastrophic contingencies

LEARNING AREAS: ANALYTICAL SKILLS: Creativity: Emotional resilience:
Proactivity: Self-knowledge

Many managers, faced with complex decisions, find themselves blocked in by
the fear of 'what if . . .?' Faced with uncertainty, doubt, and the possibility
of a bad, even catastrophic consequence to our action, we tend towards stress
and the inability to act.

This activity is designed to help you overcome this kind of blockage.

*Step 1*

Next time you are faced with a difficult problem, involving uncertainty, risk,
or doubt—write down, first, the various courses of action open to you. Then
list the worst possible things that could happen if everything went wrong.
What are the worst catastrophes that could occur?

*Step 2*

Take each catastrophy in turn and imagine that it really has happened.

How do you feel in this disastrous situation?

Is it so awful, or were your fears exaggerated?

Again, imagining that it has already happened:

What are you going to do now?

From this catastrophic situation what are your plans?

How are you going to cope with it?

What could you have done to lessen its bad effects? (Imagine yourself saying
'things wouldn't be so bad if only I . . .'.)

*Step 3*

When you have answered these questions you will probably find that:

(a) Many possible catastrophies are not really as bad as your first,
unconsidered fears.

116

(b) You have identified some of the plans and actions that you can implement to lessen either the probability of the catastrophy's occurrence, or the severity of its effects.

(c) You have prepared some contingency plans for coping with the catastrophy should it occur. These will be helpful in themselves and, by reducing the ambiguity and helplessness of the situation, you will have lessened your fear of it.

You should now be able to overcome the blockage and make your decisions.

FOLLOW-UP

When drawing up your contingency plans, Activities 27 (Action Planning), 11 (Planning Change), and 9 (Choosing Solutions with a Chance) will be helpful. If you would like to read more about formal methods of identifying and analysing contingencies, you should find *The Anatomy of Decisions* by P. G. Moore and H. Thomas (Penguin, 1976) helpful.

# Activity 14
## Scheduling*

---

LEARNING AREAS: ANALYTICAL SKILLS: Professional knowledge

Many managers are involved in scheduling work. This applies not only to production planning (involving the scheduling of work to specific machines), but also to a wide range of repair and service activities (scheduling jobs to specific workers, craftsmen, and specialists). Poor scheduling leads to delays, failure to meet targets, complaints, loss of business, excessive costs. It is therefore very important that a manager can schedule work as effectively as possible.

**The activity**

This particular activity relates to production scheduling, but the method can be adopted for other uses, such as planning work among a group of skilled craftsmen, where machines A–D are replaced by people.

You are asked to re-plan a work schedule to achieve maximum machine utilization and minimize excessive costs. The workshop contains four machines A, B, C, and D, each with eight standard hours available per day from Monday to Friday. Saturday is overtime and, if worked, four standard hours are available on each machine.

Most of the orders have to be processed on each of the machines in different sequences. The setting-up time on each machine is one hour, marked on the Gant chart, and a machine cannot be set up until the job has completed its time on the previous machine. If a job has to be removed from a machine before completion, an hour must be allowed for removal of the job before setting up the next job.

* This activity was designed by Keith Bloomfield, Lecturer in Management at Stannington College of Further Education, Sheffield, England.

118

Before scheduling, the forward loading commitment due to previous work on each machine must be marked off on Day 1.

     i.e., machine A—4 hours
                   B—6 hours
                   C—3 hours
                   D—4 hours

At the end of the exercise you are asked to calculate the excess costs as follows:

    Cost of idle time at £5 per hour.
    Cost of setting-up time at £1 per hour.
    Cost of opening the factory on Saturday including any overtime premiums at £100 per Saturday.
    Cost of late orders at £30 per day per order.
    Cost of completing orders too early at £5 per day per order.

Table A14.1 gives the list of orders to be scheduled and the necessary information about each order. It is important to remember that orders received cannot be scheduled on a day which has already passed. No part of any order received on Day 2 can be scheduled on Day 1.

| Job no. | Machine order | Time on each machine in hours | Required for day no. |
|---|---|---|---|
| *Received Day 1* | | | |
| 100 | B | 4 | |
| | A | 2 | |
| | C | 5 | |
| | D | 1 | 11 |
| 101 | B | 5 | |
| | D | 2 | |
| | A | 2 | |
| | C | 4 | 4 |
| 102 | A | 2 | |
| | C | 1 | |
| | D | 5 | 7 |
| 103 | D | 4 | |
| | C | 5 | |
| | B | 1 | |
| | A | 2 | 4 |

*Table A14.1. Order sheet*

| Job no. | Machine order | Time on each machine in hours | Required for day no. |
|---------|---------------|-------------------------------|----------------------|
| *Received Day 2* | | | |
| 104 | D | 1 | |
|     | B | 5 | |
|     | A | 3 | |
|     | C | 1 | 4 |
| 105 | C | 6 | |
|     | B | 1 | |
|     | A | 2 | |
|     | D | 4 | 11 |
| 106 | A | 1 | |
|     | D | 2 | |
|     | C | 3 | |
|     | E | 4 | 8 |
| *Received Day 3* | | | |
| 107 | A | 7 | |
|     | B | 2 | |
|     | C | 4 | 4 |
| 108 | B | 7 | |
|     | D | 4 | |
|     | B | 2 | 4 |
| *Received Day 4* | | | |
| 109 | D | 4 | |
|     | A | 2 | 5 |
| 110 | C | 1 | |
|     | B | 3 | 5 |

*Table A14.1* (Continued)

The orders in Table A14.1 have been scheduled on to the Gant chart (Table A14.2) as an example of bad scheduling.

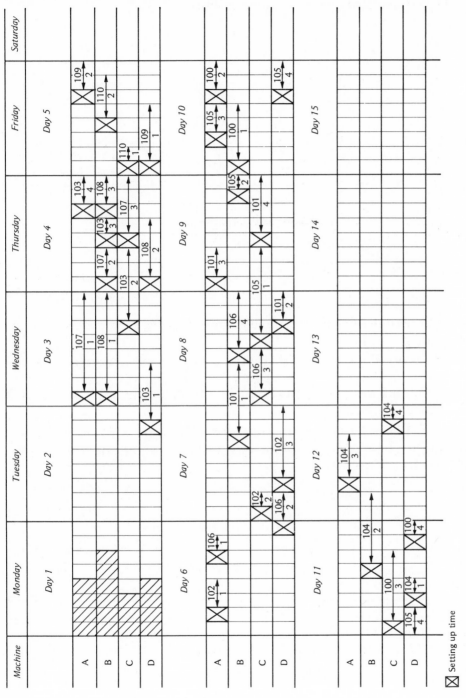

Setting up time

*Table A14.2. Sample solution—poor scheduling*

Just how bad the scheduling is on the previous Gant chart (Table A14.2), can be demonstrated by the following analysis:

*Machine utilization*

| Machine | Total time inc. Sat. if used | Running time Hours | % | Setting time hours | % | Idle time hours | % |
|---|---|---|---|---|---|---|---|
| A | 96 | 27 | 28.1 | 9 | 9.4 | 60 | 62.5 |
| B | 96 | 40 | 41.7 | 10 | 10.4 | 46 | 47.9 |
| C | 96 | 33 | 34.4 | 9 | 9.4 | 54 | 56.2 |
| D | 96 | 31 | 32.3 | 9 | 9.4 | 56 | 58.3 |
| | | 131 | | 37 | | 216 | |

*Excess costs*                                                £
    Idle time          216 hours at £5 per hour = 1080
    Setting time         37 hours at £1 per hour =   37
    Saturdays worked  NIL at £100 per Sat.     =    0
    Late orders          5 days at £30 per day  =  150
    Early orders       NIL days at £5 per day   =    0
                                                  ――――
    Total excess costs                          = 1267

*Table A14.3. Analysis sheet of Table A14.2*

It can be seen that the percentage idle time is very high and that excess costs are running at £13 per hour.

On the blank Gant chart (Table A14.5), you should now reschedule the work to try and improve machine utilization and reduce excess costs. There is also a blank analysis sheet (Table A14.4) for you to analyse your chart after completing it.

On pages 124 and 125 (Tables A14.6 and A14.7) you will find a suggested solution for rescheduling. Do not turn to this now, but use it to compare with your own solution.

*Machine utilization*

| Machine | Total time inc. Sat. if used | Running time hours | % | Setting time hours | % | Idle time hours | % |
|---|---|---|---|---|---|---|---|
| A | | | | | | | |
| B | | | | | | | |
| C | | | | | | | |
| D | | | | | | | |

*Excess costs*                                                £
    Idle time          hours at £5 per hour  =
    Setting time       hours at £1 per hour  =
    Saturdays worked   days at £100 per Sat. =
    Late orders        days at £30 per day   =
    Early orders       days at £5 per day    =
                                                  ――――
    Total excess costs                       =

*Table A14.4. Analysis sheet for your solution*

| Machine | Monday | Tuesday | Wednesday | Thursday | Friday | Saturday |
|---------|--------|---------|-----------|----------|--------|----------|
| | Day 1 | Day 2 | Day 3 | Day 4 | Day 5 | |
| A | | | | | | |
| B | | | | | | |
| C | | | | | | |
| D | | | | | | |
| | Day 6 | Day 7 | Day 8 | Day 9 | Day 10 | |
| A | | | | | | |
| B | | | | | | |
| C | | | | | | |
| D | | | | | | |
| | Day 11 | Day 12 | Day 13 | Day 14 | Day 15 | |
| A | | | | | | |
| B | | | | | | |
| C | | | | | | |
| D | | | | | | |

*Table A14.5. Blank chart for your solution*

| Machine | Monday<br>*Day 1* | Tuesday<br>*Day 2* | Wednesday<br>*Day 3* | Thursday<br>*Day 4* | Friday<br>*Day 5* | Saturday |
|---|---|---|---|---|---|---|
| A | 102 1 | 100 2 | 107 1 | 103 4 / 104 3 | 107 1 / 109 2 | 108 3 |
| B | 106 1 / 100 1 | 101 1 | 104 2 / 101 3 | 103 3 / 108 1 | 110 2 / 107 2 | 107 3 |
| C | 102 3 | 103 2 | 100 3 / 103 2 | 101 4 / 110 1 / 104 4 | 105 1 | |
| D | 103 1 | 102 3 | 104 1 / 101 2 / 100 4 | 106 2 / 109 1 | 108 2 | |

| Machine | *Day 6* | *Day 7* | *Day 8* | *Day 9* | *Day 10* | |
|---|---|---|---|---|---|---|
| A | 105 3 | | | | | |
| B | 105 2 / 106 4 | | | | | |
| C | 106 3 / 105 4 | | | | | |
| D | | | | | | |

| Machine | *Day 11* | *Day 12* | *Day 13* | *Day 14* | *Day 15* | |
|---|---|---|---|---|---|---|
| A | | | | | | |
| B | | | | | | |
| C | | | | | | |
| D | | | | | | |

*Table A14.6. Sample solution—improved scheduling*

*Machine utilization*

| Machine | Total time inc. Sat. if used | Running time hours | % | Setting time hours | % | Idle time hours | % |
|---|---|---|---|---|---|---|---|
| A | 48 | 27 | 56.2 | 10 | 20.8 | 11 | 23.0 |
| B | 52 | 39 | 75.0 | 10 | 19.2 | 3 | 5.8 |
| C | 52 | 33 | 63.5 | 11 | 21.2 | 8 | 15.3 |
| D | 48 | 30 | 62.5 | 9 | 18.8 | 9 | 18.7 |
| | | 129 | | 40 | | 31 | |

| Excess costs | | £ |
|---|---|---|
| Idle time | 31 hours at £5 per hour = | 155 |
| Setting time | 40 hours at £1 per hour = | 40 |
| Saturdays worked | 1 at £100 per Sat.   = | 100 |
| Late orders | 4 days at £30 per day = | 120 |
| Early orders | 18 days at £5 per day = | 90 |
| Total excess costs | = | 505 |

*Table A14.7. Sample improved scheduling—analysis sheet*

From the analysis in Table A14.7 it can be seen that the utilization of each machine has been almost doubled. Excess costs have been reduced to approximately £10 per hour over the 6 days scheduled. Assuming that orders would continue to come in and be scheduled on days 7 to 12, the hourly excess costs over the 12 days would probably be even lower.

While the solution may not be perfect, it demonstrates the consequences of bad scheduling and that one must always seek to maximize machine utilization.

FOLLOW-UP

If you were able to plan a much improved schedule, there's possibly not much else you need to know about Gant charts. However, you still might like to ask yourself if you are using your scheduling skills appropriately in your own job. If not, why? Also, what about other scheduling techniques?

If you were not able to devise a better schedule, you may be saying 'So what? My job doesn't involve that sort of thing.' Are you sure? Many jobs could be improved by applying this type of thinking, even if scheduling techniques seem to be of little relevance.

If you do want to know more about scheduling, whom could you ask about it in your organization? There will probably be people with specialized knowledge somewhere. If not, try the management department at your local college of further education. Or, you might like to read about it. Some recommended books are: *Production Planning* by J. L. Burbridge (Heinemann, 1971); *Production Control in Management* by D. K. Corke (Edward Arnold, 1969); *Production Management* by H. A. Harding (McDonald and Evans, 1974).

# Activity 15
## Budgetary control*

LEARNING AREAS: ANALYTICAL SKILLS: Professional knowledge

To be successful, an organization must plan the flow of money into and out of itself. This requires that objectives be set, detailed operating plans made, and monetary values attached to these plans.

In carrying out a cost control process, the manager must

1. plan income and expenditure;

2. compare actual income and expenditure with those planned;

3. take action to correct deviations.

## The activity

The intention is to give you the opportunity to test yourself in a budgetary control activity.

From the following information, and from further information contained in the exercise, complete the 12 Functional Budgets, Master Budgets, Flexible Budget, and finally the Budget Report for Quarter One.

Lynfield Limited manufactures a single product—plastic 'wizoos' which are sold for £9 per unit, the money being received three months in arrears.

Two types of machine are used in the manufacturing process: intrusion machines and polishers, costing £1 200 and £2 000 respectively to buy and install. The company currently owns 8 intrusion machines and 19 polishers, each with 480 standard hours available each quarter. Each unit of production consumes 0.2 standard hours for intrusion and 0.5 standard hours for polishing. When new machines are bought they are available for production immediately and are paid for three months in arrears.

Each 'wizoo' consumes 1.5 kg of Polyplasm which is bought in 10 000 kg lots to minimize costs. The price is £0.02 per kg and is paid for three months in arrears.

* This activity was designed by Keith Bloomfield, Lecturer in Management at Stannington College of Further Education, Sheffield, England.

126

Each machine requires one person to operate it. For every direct worker there are three indirect production workers. Each person works 40 hours per week for 48 weeks per year and the rates of pay are as follows:

Direct      £2.00 per hour
Indirect    £1.50 per hour

The company uses the straight-line method of depreciation (i.e., 10 per cent per annum on cost). First quarter depreciation is as follows:

Salesmen's cars          £200
Production buildings     £125
Offices                  £60

The fixed production overheads, which include depreciation on production buildings and production machines, are £6 000 in quarter one.

Variable production overheads are £0.50 per unit. Salesmen's commission is 1.5 per cent of sales value.

Sales commission, direct labour, indirect production costs, administration costs, and selling and distribution costs, are all paid for in the same quarter as they occur.

Finally, you are asked to budget for the purchase of an extra motor vehicle for the sales department in quarter three, to be paid for three months in arrears, at a cost of £2 500. No depreciation is to be charged against this new vehicle in this financial year.

When you have finished the exercise, compare your solution with that given, with explanations, on pages 132–137.

|  | Jan.-Mar. | Apr.-June | July-Sept. | Oct.-Dec. | Total for year |
|---|---|---|---|---|---|
| **1. SALES BUDGET** | | | | | |
| Sales quantity (units) | 10 000 | 25 000 | 30 000 | 18 000 | 83 000 |
| Sales revenue  (£) | | | | | |
| | | | | | |
| **2. MACHINE TIME BUDGET** | | | | | |
| Production (units) | 18 000 | 22 000 | 24 500 | 21 000 | 85 000 |
| Standard hours required—Intrusion machines | | | | | |
| No. of intrusion machines | | | | | |
| Standard hours required—Polishers | | | | | |
| No. of polishers | | | | | |

*Table A15.1*

|  | Jan.-<br>Mar. | Apr.-<br>June | July-<br>Sept. | Oct.-<br>Dec. | Total<br>for<br>year |
|---|---|---|---|---|---|
| **3. MACHINE UTILIZATION BUDGET** | | | | | |
| Intrusion—Hours available | | | | | |
|         Hours required | | | | | |
|         % Utilization | | | | | |
| Polishers—Hours available | | | | | |
|         Hours required | | | | | |
|         % Utilization | | | | | |
| **4. DIRECT MATERIALS BUDGET (Polyplasm)** | | | | | |
| Required minimum end stock (kilos) | 9 200 | 6 200 | 700 | 2 950 | 2 950 |
| Production requirements   (kilos) | | | | | |
| Estimated opening stock   (kilos) | 1 200 | | | | |
| Required purchases   (kilos) | | | | | |
| **5. PURCHASING BUDGET (PRODUCTION)** | | | | | |
| Direct materials   (£) | | | | | |
| Indirect production materials (£) | 250 | 400 | 600 | 500 | 1 750 |
| Maintenance materials   (£) | 200 | 220 | 270 | 220 | 910 |
| **6. LABOUR BUDGET** | | | | | |
| (a) *Direct labour* | | | | | |
| Men required—Intrusion | | | | | |
| Men required—Polishers | | | | | |
| Total men required | | | | | |
| Total hours | | | | | |
| Total cost (£) | | | | | |
| (b) *Indirect labour* | | | | | |
| Total men required | | | | | |
| Total hours | | | | | |
| Total cost (£) | | | | | |
| **7. MAINTENANCE BUDGET** | | | | | |
| Labour   (£) | 500 | 520 | 570 | 520 | 2 110 |
| Materials   (£) | 200 | 200 | 250 | 200 | 850 |
| Overheads (£) | 50 | 50 | 50 | 50 | 200 |
| Total   (£) | 750 | 770 | 870 | 770 | 3 160 |
| **8. PRODUCTION OVERHEAD BUDGET** | | | | | |
| Indirect materials   (£) | | | | | |
| Indirect labour   (£) | | | | | |
| Variable overhead   (£) | | | | | |
| Fixed overhead   (£) | | | | | |
| Maintenance   (£) | | | | | |
| Total production overhead cost (£) | | | | | |

*Table A15.1* (Continued)

|  | | Jan.-<br>Mar. | Apr.-<br>June | July-<br>Sept. | Oct.-<br>Dec. | Total<br>for<br>year |
|---|---|---|---|---|---|---|
| **9. SELLING AND DISTRIBUTION COST BUDGET** | | | | | | |
| Salesmen's salaries | (£) | 1 000 | 1 000 | 1 000 | 1 000 | 4 000 |
| Salesmen's commission | (£) | | | | | |
| Salesmen's expenses | (£) | 650 | 750 | 900 | 700 | 3 000 |
| Warehouse and distribution costs | (£) | 400 | 400 | 400 | 400 | 1 600 |
| Advertising expenditure | (£) | 100 | 1 000 | 400 | 100 | 1 600 |
| Sales office expenses | (£) | 850 | 850 | 850 | 850 | 3 400 |
| Fixed overheads (depreciation) | (£) | 200 | 200 | 200 | 200 | 800 |
| Total | (£) | | | | | |
| **10. ADMINISTRATION COST BUDGET** | | | | | | |
| Materials | (£) | 640 | 720 | 890 | 750 | 3 000 |
| Wages and salaries | (£) | 1 600 | 1 800 | 1 800 | 1 875 | 7 075 |
| Repairs | (£) | 480 | 540 | 667 | 562 | 2 249 |
| General Expenses | (£) | 480 | 540 | 668 | 563 | 2 251 |
| Fixed overhead (depreciation) | (£) | 60 | 60 | 60 | 60 | 240 |
| Total | (£) | | | | | |
| **11. CAPITAL EXPENDITURE BUDGET** | | | | | | |
| Intrusion machines | (£) | | | | | |
| Polishers | (£) | | | | | |
| Motor vehicles | (£) | | | | | |
| Total | (£) | | | | | |
| **12. CASH BUDGET** | | | | | | |
| **PAYMENTS** | | | | | | |
| Direct materials | (£) | 6 000 | | | | |
| Direct labour | (£) | | | | | |
| Production overheads | (£) | | | | | |
| Selling and distribution | (£) | | | | | |
| Administration | (£) | | | | | |
| Capital expenditure | (£) | | | | | |
| Total payments | (£) | | | | | |
| **RECEIPTS** | | | | | | |
| Sales revenue | (£) | 162 000 | | | | |
| Operating surplus<br>or deficiency | (£) | | | | | |

**13. MASTER BUDGETS**

(a) *Budgeted profit and loss account*

|  | £ | % |
|---|---|---|
| Net sales | | |
| Total production cost | | |
| Less selling and distribution costs | | |
| Administration expenses | | |
| Net profit before tax | | |

Less provision for tax (50%)

NET PROFIT

*Table A15.1* (Continued)

(b) *Budgeted balance sheet*

| FIXED ASSETS | £ | £ | £ |
|---|---|---|---|
| Land | | 200 000 | |
| Buildings | | | |
| Less depreciation to date | 925 | | |
| | | | |
| Plant and Machinery | | | |
| Intrusion machines | | | |
| Polishers | | | |
| Total value of machines | | | |
| Less depreciation to date | 5 200 | | |
| Motor vehicles | | | |
| Less depreciation to date | 800 | | |
| | | | |
| CURRENT ASSETS | | | |
| Stock | 75 000 | | |
| Debtors | 100 000 | | |
| Cash | 95 643 | | |
| | | | |
| LESS CURRENT LIABILITIES | | | |
| Creditors | 40 000 | | |
| Tax | | | |
| Dividends | 30 000 | | |

TOTAL FIXED ASSETS AND WORKING CAPITAL

| FINANCED BY | | | |
|---|---|---|---|
| Issued share capital | | 200 000 | |
| General reserve | | | |
| Profit and loss | | | |

14.  FLEXIBLE BUDGET (FULL YEAR)

| Level of activity | 80% | 90% | 100% |
|---|---|---|---|
| Units of production | 68 400 | 76 950 | 85 500 |

PRIME COSTS (£)
Direct materials
Direct labour

VARIABLE OVERHEADS (£)
Production
Salesmen's commission

*Table A15.1* (Continued)

SEMI-VARIABLE OVERHEADS (£)

| | | |
|---|---|---|
| Indirect materials | 1 575 | 1 662 |
| Indirect labour | 260 496 | 274 968 |
| Maintenance costs | 2 844 | 3 002 |
| Salesmen's expenses | 2 700 | 2 850 |

FIXED OVERHEADS (£)

Production
Salesmen's salaries
Warehouse and distribution costs
Advertising
Sales office expenses
Other sales fixed overheads
Administration

TOTAL COSTS (£)

## 15. THE BUDGET REPORT—QUARTER ONE

| Element of cost | Budget 90% Level | Actual | Variance Favourable | Adverse |
|---|---|---|---|---|
| **PRIME COSTS (£)** | | | | |
| Direct materials | | 5 508 | | |
| Direct labour | | 29 000 | | |
| **VARIABLE OVERHEADS (£)** | | | | |
| Production | | 9 500 | | |
| Salesmen's commission | | 2 261 | | |
| **SEMI-VARIABLE OVERHEADS (£)** | | | | |
| Indirect materials | | 600 | | |
| Indirect labour | | 68 700 | | |
| Maintenance costs | | 700 | | |
| Salesmen's expenses | | 600 | | |
| **FIXED OVERHEADS (£)** | | | | |
| Production | | 6 320 | | |
| Salesmen's salaries | | 1 000 | | |
| Warehouse and distributions costs | | 380 | | |
| Advertising | | 400 | | |
| Sales office expenses | | 800 | | |
| Other sales fixed overheads | | 200 | | |
| Administration costs | | 3 904 | | |
| TOTAL COSTS (£) | | 129 873 | | |

*Table A15.1* (Continued)

Explanation of the solution given in Table A15.2

*Budget No.*

2    The number of machines required is calculated to the nearest whole machine upwards (i.e., 7.2 machines would be 8).

3    The hours available are based on the number of machines required as stated in Budget 2.

5    Direct materials are taken from the required purchases in Budget 4. To satisfy minimum end stock requirements it is necessary to purchase at least 35 000 kilos in quarter one. To minimize cost, 40 000 kilos is therefore ordered.

8    The increases in fixed overheads from quarter one to quarter two and quarter two to quarter three are due to the extra depreciation required on the new intrusion and polishing machines.

11    Remember that new machines are paid for three months in arrears.

12    Production overheads are calculated from the total production overhead cost in Budget 8 less depreciation on machines and production buildings, e.g., quarter one.

Production overheads (cash budget) = £74 320 − £1 190 (machine depreciation) − £125 (building depreciation).

Similarly, the total selling and distribution costs include £200 depreciation which has to be deducted from the figure entered into the cash budget, and the total administration costs include £60 depreciation which also has to be deducted before entry to cash budget.

13a    Percentage figures are calculated as a percentage of the net sales.

13b    The original value of buildings can be calculated from the amount of depreciation charged, at an annual rate of 10 per cent. i.e., £185 per quarter x 4 x 10 = £7 400

Original value of the machines—
11 intrusion at £1 200
26 polishers at £2 000
Total value £65 200

Motor vehicles original value—
£200 x 4 x 10 = £8 000
plus new vehicle purchased in third quarter at £2 500
Total value £10 500

On the liabilities side of the balance sheet the general reserve figure is calculated by difference.

(Continued on page 137)

| | Jan.-Mar.- | Apr.-June | July-Sept. | Oct.-Dec. | Total for Year |
|---|---|---|---|---|---|
| **1. SALES BUDGET** | | | | | |
| Sales quantity (units) | 10 000 | 25 000 | 30 000 | 18 000 | 83 000 |
| Sales revenue   (£) | 90 000 | 225 000 | 270 000 | 162 000 | 747 000 |
| **2. MACHINE TIME BUDGET** | | | | | |
| Production (units) | 18 000 | 22 000 | 24 500 | 21 000 | 85 500 |
| Standard hours required— | | | | | |
| Intrusion machines | 3 600 | 4 400 | 4 900 | 4 200 | 17 100 |
| No. of intrusion machines | 8 | 10 | 11 | 11 | — |
| Standard hours required— | | | | | |
| Polishers | 9 000 | 11 000 | 12 250 | 10 500 | 42 750 |
| No. of polishers | 19 | 23 | 26 | 26 | — |
| **3. MACHINE UTILIZATION BUDGET** | | | | | |
| Intrusion—Hours available | 3 840 | 4 800 | 5 280 | 5 280 | — |
| Hours required | 3 600 | 4 400 | 4 900 | 4 200 | — |
| % Utilization | 93.75 | 91.66 | 92.80 | 79.54 | — |
| Polishers—Hours available | 9 120 | 11 040 | 12 480 | 12 480 | — |
| Hours required | 9 000 | 11 000 | 12 250 | 10 500 | — |
| % Utilization | 98.68 | 99.63 | 98.15 | 84.13 | — |
| **4. DIRECT MATERIALS BUDGET (Polyplasm)** | | | | | |
| Required min. end stock (kilos) | 9 200 | 6 200 | 700 | 2 950 | 2 950 |
| Production requirements (kilos) | 27 000 | 33 000 | 36 750 | 31 500 | 128 250 |
| Estimated opening stock (kilos) | 1 200 | 9 200 | 6 200 | 700 | 1 200 |
| Required purchases       (kilos) | 35 000 | 30 000 | 31 250 | 33 750 | 130 000 |
| **5. PURCHASING BUDGET (PRODUCTION)** | | | | | |
| Direct materials              (£) | 8 000 | 6 000 | 6 000 | 6 000 | 26 000 |
| Indirect production materials (£) | 250 | 400 | 600 | 500 | 1 750 |
| Maintenance materials        (£) | 200 | 220 | 270 | 220 | 910 |
| **6. LABOUR BUDGET** | | | | | |
| (a) *Direct labour* | | | | | |
| Men required—Intrusion | 8 | 10 | 11 | 11 | — |
| Men required—Polishers | 19 | 23 | 26 | 26 | — |
| Total men required | 27 | 33 | 37 | 37 | — |
| Total hours | 12 960 | 15 840 | 17 760 | 17 760 | 64 320 |
| Total cost (£) | 25 920 | 31 680 | 35 520 | 35 520 | 128 640 |
| (b) *Indirect labour* | | | | | |
| Total men required | 81 | 99 | 111 | 111 | — |
| Total hours | 38 880 | 47 520 | 53 280 | 53 280 | 192 960 |
| Total cost (£) | 58 320 | 71 280 | 79 920 | 79 920 | 289 440 |
| **7. MAINTENANCE BUDGET** | | | | | |
| Labour    (£) | 500 | 520 | 570 | 520 | 2 110 |
| Materials (£) | 200 | 200 | 250 | 200 | 850 |
| Overheads (£) | 50 | 50 | 50 | 50 | 200 |
| Total      (£) | 750 | 770 | 870 | 770 | 3 160 |

*Table A15.2*

|  |  | Jan.-Mar.- | Apr.-June | July-Sept. | Oct.-Dec. | Total for Year |
|---|---|---|---|---|---|---|
| **8. PRODUCTION OVERHEAD BUDGET** |  |  |  |  |  |  |
| Indirect materials | (£) | 250 | 400 | 600 | 500 | 1 750 |
| Indirect labour | (£) | 58 320 | 71 280 | 79 920 | 79 920 | 289 440 |
| Variable overheads | (£) | 9 000 | 11 000 | 12 250 | 10 500 | 42 750 |
| Fixed overheads | (£) | 6 000 | 6260 | 6 440 | 6 440 | 25 140 |
| Maintenance | (£) | 750 | 770 | 870 | 770 | 3 160 |
| Total production overheads | (£) | 74 320 | 89 710 | 100 080 | 98 130 | 362 240 |
| **9. SELLING AND DISTRIBUTION COST BUDGET** |  |  |  |  |  |  |
| Salesmen's salaries | (£) | 1 000 | 1 000 | 1 000 | 1 000 | 4 000 |
| Salesmen's commission | (£) | 1 350 | 3 375 | 4 050 | 2 430 | 11 205 |
| Salesmen's expenses | (£) | 650 | 750 | 900 | 700 | 3 000 |
| Warehouse and distribution costs | (£) | 400 | 400 | 400 | 400 | 1 600 |
| Advertising expenditure | (£) | 100 | 1 000 | 400 | 100 | 1 600 |
| Sales office expenses | (£) | 850 | 850 | 850 | 850 | 3 400 |
| Fixed overheads (depreciation) | (£) | 200 | 200 | 200 | 200 | 800 |
| Total | (£) | 4 550 | 7 575 | 7 800 | 5 680 | 25 605 |
| **10. ADMINISTRATION COST BUDGET** |  |  |  |  |  |  |
| Materials | (£) | 640 | 720 | 890 | 750 | 3 000 |
| Wages and salaries | (£) | 1 600 | 1 800 | 1 800 | 1 875 | 7 075 |
| Repairs | (£) | 480 | 540 | 667 | 562 | 2 249 |
| General expenses | (£) | 480 | 540 | 668 | 563 | 2 251 |
| Fixed overheads (depreciation) | (£) | 60 | 60 | 60 | 60 | 240 |
| Total | (£) | 3 260 | 3 660 | 4 085 | 3 810 | 14 815 |
| **11. CAPITAL EXPENDITURE BUDGET** |  |  |  |  |  |  |
| Intrusion machines | (£) | — | 2 400 | 1 200 | — | 3 600 |
| Polishers | (£) | — | 8 000 | 6 000 | — | 14 000 |
| Motor vehicles | (£) | — | — | 2 500 | — | 2 500 |
| Total | (£) | — | 10 400 | 9 700 | — | 20 100 |
| **12. CASH BUDGET** |  |  |  |  |  |  |
| **PAYMENTS (£)** |  |  |  |  |  |  |
| Direct materials |  | 6 000 | 8 000 | 6 000 | 6 000 | 26 000 |
| Direct labour |  | 25 920 | 31 680 | 35 520 | 35 520 | 128 640 |
| Production overheads |  | 73 005 | 88 135 | 98 325 | 96 375 | 355 840 |
| Selling and distribution |  | 4 350 | 7 375 | 7 600 | 5 480 | 24 805 |
| Administration |  | 3 200 | 3 600 | 4 025 | 3 750 | 14 575 |
| Capital expenditure |  | — | — | 10 400 | 9 700 | 20 100 |
| Total payments |  | 112 475 | 138 790 | 161 870 | 156 825 | 569 960 |
| **RECEIPTS (£)** |  |  |  |  |  |  |
| Sales revenue |  | 162 000 | 90 000 | 225 000 | 270 000 | 747 000 |
| Operating surplus or deficiency |  | 49 525 | (48 790) | 63 130 | 113 175 | 177 040 |

*Table A15.2* (Continued)

### 13. MASTER BUDGETS
(a) *Budgeted profit and loss account*

|  | £ | % |
|---|---|---|
| Net sales | 747 000 | 100 |
| Total production costs | 516 530 | 69.1 |
|  | 230 470 | 30.9 |
| Less selling and distribution costs | 25 605 | 3.4 |
| Administration expenses | 14 815 | 2.0 |
|  | 40 420 | 5.4 |
| Net profit before tax | 190 050 | 25.4 |
| Less provision for tax (50%) | 95 025 | 12.7 |
| NET PROFIT | 95 025 | 12.7 |

(b) *Budgeted balance sheet*

| FIXED ASSETS | £ | £ | £ |
|---|---|---|---|
| Land |  | 200 000 |  |
| Buildings | 7 400 |  |  |
| Less depreciation to date | 925 | 6 475 |  |
| Plant and machinery |  |  |  |
| Intrusion machines | 13 200 |  |  |
| Polishers | 52 000 |  |  |
| Total value of machines | 65 200 |  |  |
| Less depreciation to date | 5 200 | 60 000 |  |
| Motor vehicles | 10 500 |  |  |
| Less depreciation to date | 800 | 9 700 | 276 175 |
| CURRENT ASSETS |  |  |  |
| Stock | 75 000 |  |  |
| Debtors | 100 000 |  |  |
| Cash | 95 643 | 270 643 |  |
| LESS CURRENT LIABILITIES |  |  |  |
| Creditors | 40 000 |  |  |
| Tax | 95 025 |  |  |
| Dividends | 30 000 | 165 025 | 105 618 |
| TOTAL FIXED ASSETS AND WORKING CAPITAL |  |  | 381 793 |
| FINANCED BY |  |  |  |
| Issued share capital |  | 200 000 |  |
| General reserve |  | 86 768 |  |
| Profit and loss |  | 95 025 |  |
|  |  |  | 381 793 |

*Table A15.2* (Continued)

## 14.  FLEXIBLE BUDGET (FULL YEAR)

| | | | |
|---|---|---|---|
| Level of activity | 80% | 90% | 100% |
| Units of production | 68 400 | 76 950 | 85 500 |

**PRIME COSTS (£)**

| | | | |
|---|---|---|---|
| Direct materials | 20 520 | 23 085 | 25 650 |
| Direct labour | 102 912 | 115 776 | 128 640 |
| | 123 432 | 138 861 | 154 290 |

**VARIABLE OVERHEADS (£)**

| | | | |
|---|---|---|---|
| Production | 34 200 | 38 475 | 42 750 |
| Salesmen's commission | 8 964 | 10 085 | 11 205 |

**SEMI-VARIABLE OVERHEADS (£)**

| | | | |
|---|---|---|---|
| Indirect materials | 1 575 | 1 662 | 1 750 |
| Indirect labour | 260 496 | 274 968 | 289 440 |
| Maintenance costs | 2 844 | 3 002 | 3 160 |
| Salesmen's expenses | 2 700 | 2 850 | 3 000 |
| | 310 779 | 331 042 | 351 305 |

**FIXED OVERHEADS (£)**

| | | | |
|---|---|---|---|
| Production | 25 140 | 25 140 | 25 140 |
| Salesmen's salaries | 4 000 | 4 000 | 4 000 |
| Warehouse and distribution costs | 1 600 | 1 600 | 1 600 |
| Advertising | 1 600 | 1 600 | 1 600 |
| Sales office expenses | 3 400 | 3 400 | 3 400 |
| Other sales fixed overheads | 800 | 800 | 800 |
| Administration costs | 14 815 | 14 815 | 14 815 |
| | 51 355 | 51 355 | 51 355 |

| | | | |
|---|---|---|---|
| TOTAL COSTS (£) | 485 566 | 521 258 | 556 950 |

## 15.  THE BUDGET REPORT—QUARTER ONE

| | Budget 90% Level | Actual | Variance Favourable | Adverse |
|---|---|---|---|---|
| **PRIME COSTS (£)** | | | | |
| Direct materials | 5771 | 5 508 | 263 | |
| Direct labour | 28 944 | 29 000 | | (56) |
| **VARIABLE OVERHEADS (£)** | | | | |
| Production | 9 619 | 9 500 | 119 | |
| Salesmen's commission | 2 521 | 2 261 | 260 | |
| **SEMI-VARIABLE OVERHEADS (£)** | | | | |
| Indirect materials | 416 | 600 | | (184) |
| Indirect labour | 68 742 | 68 700 | 42 | |
| Maintenance costs | 751 | 700 | 51 | |
| Salesmen's expenses | 713 | 600 | 113 | |

*Table A15.2* (Continued)

| FIXED OVERHEADS (£) | | | | |
|---|---|---|---|---|
| Production | 6 285 | 6 320 | | (35) |
| Salesmen's salaries | 1 000 | 1 000 | — | — |
| Warehouse and distribution costs | 400 | 380 | 20 | — |
| Advertising | 400 | 400 | — | — |
| Sales office expenses | 850 | 800 | 50 | — |
| Other sales fixed overheads | 200 | 200 | — | — |
| Administration costs | 3 704 | 3 904 | | (200) |
| TOTAL COSTS (£) | 130 316 | 129 873 | 443 | |

*Table A15.2* (Continued)

14    The budget figures for the 100 per cent level of activity can be obtained directly from Budgets 4 (Direct Materials—128 250 kilos at £0.20 per kilo), 6a, 8, 9, and 10. In the case of prime costs and variable costs the 80 and 90 per cent levels can be calculated, the semi-variable overheads are given, and the fixed overheads remain the same at all levels of activity.

15    The budget figures are one-quarter of the figures in the 90 per cent column in Budget 14.

FOLLOW-UP

If you have done the exercise correctly, there is not much more specific knowledge you are likely to need on budgetary control techniques. Even so, you might ask yourself if you are making full and appropriate use of your knowledge in your job. If not, what else could you be doing?

If you have not been able to do the exercise, you might feel it doesn't matter, that your job doesn't involve this sort of thing. If so, think hard about this. Your job might not involve you in this sort of activity at the moment—but perhaps it should? Even if you don't have to prepare detailed budgets, shouldn't you be applying budgetary-type thinking to what you do? Who does prepare budgets? Can you understand those that are prepared? Who's budgetary hand is on the tiller of your department?

If you would like a better understanding of these techniques, a number of sources are available. Perhaps the best of these would be relevant colleagues in your own organization who could explain things to you. (If you don't know who these people are—find out.)

Alternatively, you may be able to get guidance from your local college of further education, either through a special course, or by consulting appropriate staff.

Finally, some recommended books on this subject are: *Management Accounting* by W. M. Harper (McDonald and Evans, 1974); *Introduction to Accounting for Business Studies* by F. T. Langley (Butterworth, 1973); *Principles and Practice of Management Accounting* by J. L. Brown and L. R. Howard (McDonald and Evans, 1969).

# Activity 16
## Response to conflict

---

LEARNING AREAS: SOCIAL SKILLS: Emotional resilience: Sensitivity to events

Some of the important parts of a manager's job are concerned with conflict. He may be called upon to mediate between two individuals in conflict. He may be in conflict himself with another manager who is competing for the same resources or for the ear of a superior. He will be continually handling crises—unforeseen events caused by breakdowns, absenteeism, loss of supplies, lack of buyers, and so on.

All these are conflict situations where one party is frustrating the goals of another party and, yet, they are dependent on each other. The outcomes can be many and varied, from outright battling through negotiations and compromise, to walk-overs or avoidance. In particular situations one response might be more appropriate than another, but no one response is correct every time.

Stop and think about your own response tendency to conflict situations. How do you generally react when faced with frustration and antagonism? This activity aims to get you to look at your habitual or preferred response to conflict situations. It also asks you to generate alternatives to these habitual responses.

The more aware you are of your personal style, and the more ways you see of being able to resolve a particular conflict, the more sensitive, flexible, and successful you will be in coping with the problem.

There are three parts to this activity. Part 1 consists of three short case studies which invite you to place yourself in particular conflict situations. Part 2 contains a simple model of conflict resolution styles and asks you to classify yourself within the model. Part 3 is a paired comparison questionnaire which provides another way of examining your preferred approach to resolving conflict. Taken together, the three parts will build up a picture of the way you react in conflict situations, and provide a basis for more appropriate responses. Each part is complete in itself and can be tackled separately from the others.

### Activity.    Part 1: Three case studies

After each of the three short case studies, write down what your first reaction would be to that situation. Think yourself into the situation and feel the anger and frustration well up inside you.

*Case 1*

You have just arrived at the canteen and are waiting for your coffee. Across the room you see a fellow manager with whom you got into a violent row at the last management meeting. The argument concerned the shortage of skilled clerical staff—you believe your department is failing to get its fair share and that his is overstaffed. This morning one of your departmental secretaries failed to report for work and on applying to the pool you were told that the last of the 'temps' had gone to your fellow manager's department. At the sight of him, your anger and sense of injustice flood back.

What do you do? (Write down your first reaction.)

*Case 2*

The road you live on has a fringe of lawn between the footpath and the road. You look after your section and like to see it looking green and well tended. Most of your neighbours do the same, but on one side of you is a chap you don't know too well and who ignores this common policy. He never cuts the verge and he and his friends frequently park their cars on it. Recently, they have been parking on your section and, in the recent wet weather, tyre marks marred the green surface. You have spoken to him twice about this but he appears off-hand and indifferent to your concern.

One Sunday morning you wake up at 5 a.m. to the revving of engines and on looking outside see two deep scars across your lawn.

At 9 o'clock and still seething, you bump into your neighbour in the papershop.

What do you do? (Write down your first reaction.)

*Case 3*

You are a junior manager in the sales section of a very large industry. Your boss sends for you one morning and you hear on the grapevine that he's going to ask you to take on an unpopular duty that involves coming in every other Saturday. You don't like it—your wife expects you to be around for shopping, etc. on Saturdays, and you feel you are getting a raw deal because you are junior. You're on your way to the boss's office.

What do you do? (Write down your first reaction.)

When you've responded to these three cases go back over them and see if you can think of *alternative* approaches.

*Case 1. Alternative approaches*

*Case 2.  Alternative approaches*

*Case 3.  Alternative approaches*

One of the consequences of conflict is that it leads to stress, the hardening of attitudes, and a tendency to be rigid. This is why we have habitual ways of reacting to conflict situations.

   —Looking back over your initial reactions to the three cases, can you spot an habitual mode of response?

   —Think of conflicts you have had in the past with your wife, colleagues, parents, etc. Do these show any pattern of response?

   —On the three cases, how many alternatives to each of your initial responses could you generate? Two? Three? Four? or more?

The more alternatives you generated to each situation—the more likely you are to behave flexibly in practice.

## Part 2: A conflict style model

Figure A16.1[1] shows five conflict-resolving modes or styles. These are arrived at from the two basic dimensions of conflict situations. In any conflict between two parties the mode of resolution depends upon:

(a) how assertive or unassertive each party is in pursuing its own goals;

(b) how cooperative or uncooperative each party is in pursuing the goals of the other.

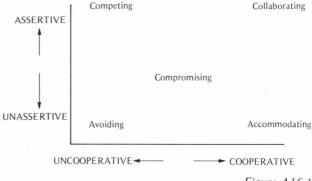

*Figure A16.1*

If both parties are highly assertive with regard to their own goals and uncooperative in terms of each others' goals then they will adopt a battling, *competing* style which is typical sometimes of union/management negotiations and husband/wife arguments. If the parties are unassertive of their own goals and still uncooperative, they will tend to avoid the conflict altogether and try to pretend it doesn't exist.

What often happens is that parties adopt different styles or modes of resolution in a particular conflict. This will then produce a joint mode which lies between any of the five polar modes on the graph. Resolving conflict is an interactive situation in which styles are mutually reciprocal. The style you adopt will affect the style your opponent adopts, and vice versa.

Try using Fig. A16.1 to diagnose a particular conflict situation in which you have personally been involved. (A personal relationship offers most scope.)

Can you fit the adopted modes of the two parties on the chart, and arrive at a description of the joint style of resolution?

Do this with as many conflict situations as you can think of. Research suggests that the appropriate style of resolving conflicts varies with such contingent issues as power, urgency, and specificity of goal. However, by diagnosing your habitual responses in certain situations and observing the responses these produce in others, you can obtain a clearer picture of yourself.

When do you avoid conflict?

When do you compete with others?

Do you ever collaborate in conflict situations?

How do you feel when you accommodate to others?

How often do you secure compromises?

The clearer you can identify your own style(s) and the responses generated in others, the more alternatives you can see in any particular situation, the more likely you are to behave appropriately the next time conflict arises.

## Part 3:  Conflict management questionnaire

This questionnaire is designed to help you further identify your preferred style of conflict resolution.

Choose from 30 pairs of statements the one in each case which best fits your preferred style of handling differences between you and others:

1.  1.  I am usually firm in pursuing my goals.
    2.  I attempt to get all concerns and issues immediately out in the open.

2.  1.  I put my cards on the table and invite the other person to do likewise.
    2.  When conflicts arise I try to win my case.

3.  1.  Once I adopt a position I defend it strongly.
    2.  I prefer not to argue but to look for the best solution possible.

4.  1.  I sometimes sacrifice my own wishes for the wishes of the other person.
    2.  I feel that differences are not always worth worrying about.

5.  1.  I accept the views of the other, rather than rock the boat.
    2.  I avoid people with strong views.

6.  1.  I like to cooperate with others and follow their ideas.
    2.  I feel that most things are not worth arguing about. I stick to my own views.

7.  1.  I try to find some compromise situation.
    2.  I am usually firm in pursuing my goals.

8.  1.  When conflicts arise I try to win my case.
    2.  I propose a middle ground.

9.  1.  I like to meet the other person half-way.
    2.  Once I adopt a position I defend it strongly.

10. 1. I feel that differences are not always worth worrying about.
    2. I try to find a compromise solution.

11. 1. I propose a middle ground.
    2. I avoid people with strong views.

12. 1. I feel that most things are not worth arguing about. I stick to my own views.
    2. I like to meet the other person half-way.

13. 1. I am usually firm in pursuing my goals.
    2. I sometimes sacrifice my own wishes for the wishes of the other person.

14. 1. I accept the views of the other, rather than rock the boat.
    2. When conflicts arise I try to win my case.

15. 1. Once I adopt a position I defend it strongly.
    2. I like to cooperate with others and follow their ideas.

16. 1. I try to find a compromise solution.
    2. I sometimes sacrifice my own wishes for the wishes of the other person.

17. 1. I would accept the views of the other, rather than rock the boat.
    2. I propose a middle ground.

18. 1. I like to meet the other person half-way.
    2. I like to cooperate with others and follow their ideas.

19. 1. I feel that differences are not always worth worrying about.
    2. I am usually firm in pursuing my goals.

20. 1. When conflicts arise I try to win my case.
    2. I avoid people with strong views.

21. 1. I feel that most things are not worth arguing about. I stick to my own views.
    2. Once I adopt a position I defend it strongly.

22. 1. I attempt to get all concerns and issues immediately out in the open.
    2. I feel that differences are not always worth worrying about.

23. 1. I avoid people with strong views.
    2. I put my cards on the table and invite the other person to do likewise.

24. 1. I prefer not to argue but to look for the best solution possible.
    2. I feel that most things are not worth arguing about. I stick to my own views.

25. 1. I attempt to get all concerns and issues immediately out in the open.
    2. I try to find a compromise solution.

26. 1. I put my cards on the table and invite the other person to do likewise.
    2. I propose a middle ground.

27. 1. I prefer not to argue but I look for the best solution possible.
    2. I like to meet the other person half-way.

28. 1. I sometimes sacrifice my own wishes for the wishes of the other person.
    2. I attempt to get all concerns and issues immediately out in the open.

29. 1. I put my cards on the table and invite the other person to do likewise.
    2. I would accept the views of others, rather than rock the boat.

30. 1. I like to cooperate with others and follow their ideas.
    2. I prefer not to argue but to look for the best possible solution.

SCORING

The questionnaire consists of three statements measuring each of the five conflict-resolving styles discussed above. Each statement is paired in comparison with one statement from each of the other four styles.

The key below shows you how to score your questionnaire. A, B, C, D, and E represent the five conflict-resolving styles as follows:

> A = Avoiding
> B = Accommodating
> C = Compromising
> D = Competing
> E = Collaborating.

So, for example, if you chose the second statement of the first pair then you would score 1 for E. If you chose the first statement of the second pair you would score another 1 for E, and so on.

The maximum score for any mode is 12 and the total aggregate score is 30. A score of more than 6 on any mode would indicate a preference for that mode, while a score of less than 6 would indicate relative neglect.

Clearly this is a one-point-in-time measure of your reaction to conflict situations, and should not be treated as having great validity. The best way to use it is to see it as a corroborative device for your own perception of your preferred style and the results you got from the cases earlier in this exercise.

| Statement pair | Conflict resolution mode | | | | |
|---|---|---|---|---|---|
| | A | B | C | D | E |
| 1 | | | | 1 | 2 |
| 2 | | | | 2 | 1 |
| 3 | | | | 1 | 2 |
| 4 | 2 | 1 | | | |
| 5 | 2 | 1 | | | |
| 6 | 2 | 1 | | | |
| 7 | | | 1 | 2 | |
| 8 | | | 2 | 1 | |
| 9 | | | 1 | 2 | |
| 10 | 1 | | 2 | | |
| 11 | 2 | | 1 | | |
| 12 | 1 | | 2 | | |
| 13 | | 2 | | 1 | |
| 14 | | 1 | | 2 | |
| 15 | | 2 | | 1 | |
| 16 | | 2 | 1 | | |
| 17 | | 1 | 2 | | |
| 18 | | 2 | 1 | | |
| 19 | 1 | | | 2 | |
| 20 | 2 | | | 1 | |
| 21 | 1 | | | 2 | |
| 22 | 2 | | | | 1 |
| 23 | 1 | | | | 2 |
| 24 | 2 | | | | 1 |
| 25 | | | 2 | | 1 |
| 26 | | | 2 | | 1 |
| 27 | | | 2 | | 1 |
| 28 | | 1 | | | 2 |
| 29 | | 2 | | | 1 |
| 30 | | 1 | | | 2 |
| TOTALS | | | | | |

*Table A16.1*

If all three of these—your perception, responses to the cases, and the questionnaire score—point in the same direction then a conclusion is comparatively simple. More uneven results will require puzzling out. As usual other people's opinions are useful additional data—particularly those with whom you have been in conflict!

## FOLLOW-UP

You need practice and application if you are to develop further your skills in resolving conflicts. Apart from what you can do by yourself, this is not an easy area in which to find courses or books. One good, easily available book is *Management of Change and Conflict* edited by J. M. Thomas and W. G. Bennis (Penguin, 1972), especially chapters 1, 13, 14, 15, 16, 17, 18. The opening chapter considers social conflict in its widest sense, but the later chapters concentrate on the foci, effects and management of conflict in organizations.

However, the best way to learn will be from your own experiences. Activities such as 'Personal Journal' (Activity 6) and 'Analysis of Experiences' (Activity 12) are designed to help you learn in this way and could well be applied to conflict experiences.

REFERENCES

1. Figure A16.1 is modelled on the ideas of R. R. Blake, and J. S. Mouton, *The Managerial Grid*, Gulf Publishing Company, 1964.

# Activity 17
## Practising new group behaviours

LEARNING AREAS: SOCIAL SKILLS: Sensitivity to events: Analytical skills:
Proactivity

Have you ever stopped to think how much of your time at work is spent in groups? Work groups, coffee groups, social groups, project teams, committees for this, that, and the other, probably account for over half your time at work. The needs and demands for increased participation and shared leadership in modern organizations mean that most of us will spend even more time in groups.

How many times have we said . . . 'Oh no! Not another meeting!' We all experience meetings which take up too much of our valuable time; meetings which seem to go round and round in circles and end inconclusively; meetings which produce arguments and bad feelings, meetings which drag on boringly. These are good reasons for taking a critical look at what happens within groups and meetings.

Groups are used for many vital functions—reaching agreements; building concensus on an issue; exchanging information; selling ideas; making decisions; coordinating disparate activities. Unfortunately, what marks many meetings is the little time actually spent on work activity and the large amount of time spent on fighting, bitching, points-scoring, backscratching, and non-work related behaviour. Often the decision facing a group is a difficult one, perhaps involving members who stand to lose or gain resources or prestige as a result. Sometimes the information to be transmitted is controversial; perhaps, instead of selling ideas, each member of the group takes up time trying to sell himself. In these situations, achieving the group objective takes a back seat, gets very blurred—people leaving the meeting ask each other what it was all about.

In situations like this, commonplace in all large organizations, and more of a problem the more 'democratic' an organization becomes, the office historian can be forgiven for reminding us that 'this wouldn't have happened in old so-and-so's day'. Unfortunately 'old so-and-so' doesn't have the solution to the present organizational predicament; his management style passed away with him. The dilemma of increased organizational democracy versus the need for efficient management makes group decision making vital. The clear indication for every manager is to learn more about how groups work; how he himself behaves in a group situation; the effect this has on others; the effect they have on him. The more we can understand behaviour in groups, the more we can control it and harness it to achieve group goals.

The purpose of this activity is to give you some practise at observing group behaviour and also offers an opportunity to experiment with your own behaviour. The more you use the framework presented here in future meetings and groups, the more you will become aware of your own behavioural tendencies and those of others.

### Activity.    Part 1: Measuring the contribution rate

As a short and simple exercise to get you started on group observation and analysis, try taking a 'contribution count' at your next meeting. You will need a 10- or 15-minute period for this, when you can concentrate on observing and are not being called on to contribute.

On a sheet of paper write the names or identifying marks for members of the group. For the next 10 to 15 minutes, note each contribution made by every group member by putting a mark beside his name. In the example given in Fig. A17.1 a 'five-barred gate method' was used:

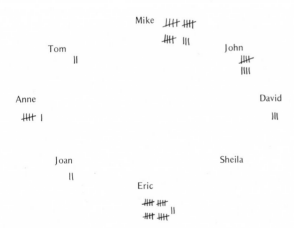

*Figure A17.1*

A 'contribution' is any spoken comment to the group (not an aside to another member) although it may be directed at one person in particular. It may be short or long, although I often put two marks for a contribution of more than, say, 30 seconds.

In Fig. A17.1 you can see clear differences between the group members in terms of the number of contributions made:

| | | |
|---|---|---|
| Eric | 22 | HIGH contributors |
| Mike | 18 | |
| John | 9 | MEDIUM contributors |
| Anne | 6 | |
| David | 3 | |
| Tom | 2 | LOW contributors |
| Joan | 2 | |
| Sheila | 0 | |

Now, why did Eric and Mike contribute most? Because they have the most to say, or because they are the more senior? If it was for either of these reasons, their dominance was probably not helping the group move towards its goals. If they spoke most because they knew most about the subject under discussion, or because they were the two principal speakers for and against an idea, then this would probably help the group achieve its goals.

What about David, Tom, Joan, and poor Sheila? Did they really have nothing to contribute, or were they shut out, asleep, junior, 'unlistened-to' members, or simply not trying?

A contribution count tells you a great deal about a group, especially if you follow it through a number of meetings. The usual pattern is that some members are habitually high contributors and some habitually low and medium, irrespective of the needs of a particular meeting. Behaviour patterns form quickly and we tend to conform to these—although this is done at a subconscious level of which we are not fully aware unless it is brought to our attention.

Share your contribution count with the other members of your group—although you will have to have a very good relationship with them to do this! If a group takes notice of this sort of observation, it can provoke changes in behaviour.

Obviously a contribution count measures only a fraction of what goes on in a group situation, and it should not be taken for more than it is. It takes no account of the *quality* of the contribution; no account of non-verbal behaviour; no account of the requirements of the particular situation; no account of how people are feeling, and so on.

It has the advantage of being an easy thing to do, and it should encourage you to observe and log:

—Who talks to whom. Who do they direct their remarks at and look at when they speak?

—Who interrupts whom?

—Who finally makes the decision—one person, two persons, the whole group?

These are more difficult to measure but will give you useful data for your own reflection and, if you can introduce it, for the greater effectiveness of the group.

## Part 2: Categorizing behaviour in groups

The effectiveness of groups depends largely upon right behaviour at the right time. When a group is indecisive and bogged down, a clear proposal will often rejuvenate and reorient it; when several proposals are already on the

| Category | Definition |
|---|---|
| Proposing | —a behaviour which puts forward a new concept, suggestion, or course of action: 'I suggest we call a meeting of all Department employees'. |
| Giving information | —a behaviour which offers facts, opinions, or clarification to others: 'There is a full definition of this in the handbook'. |
| Seeking information | —a behaviour which seeks facts, opinions, or clarification from others: 'What do the rest of you think?'. |
| Supporting/building | —a behaviour which declares support or agreement with another person or attempts to extend or develop a proposal made by another person: 'I agree with Tom and moreover we should start now'. |
| Disagreeing | —a behaviour which involves a direct criticism, difference of opinion, or disagreement with another person or his ideas: 'No, my boss would never accept a reduction in his budget'. |
| Defending/attacking | —a behaviour which attacks another person or defends an individual's own position. More emotional than disagreeing: 'That is a stupid idea' or 'My idea is better than that'. |
| Blocking/difficulty stating | —a behaviour which blocks another proposal without offering alternatives and without reasons: 'It won't work' or 'We can't have that'. |
| Testing understanding | —a behaviour which checks and seeks to establish whether an earlier contribution has been understood: 'Can I just ask you John, did you imply that you were supporting or not supporting Jim's proposal?'. |
| Summarizing | —a behaviour which summarizes, or restates concisely, the content of a previous proposal or discussion: 'Well, so far gentlemen, we have heard two proposals: Tom's—to call a meeting immediately; and John's—to delay action until next week'. |

*Table A17.1*

table, a fresh one will serve to complicate, irritate, and delay.

The categories of group behaviour shown in Table A17.1 have been developed and pioneered in this country by Neil Rackham and have been used to improve group effectiveness by British Airways, International Computers Limited, Rank Xerox International, and many other organizations.

We have chosen just eight categories with which you can practise. There are other categories, but it is confusing and difficult to work with too many.

Choose 10- to 15-minute periods in meetings to observe. This will allow concentration and yet not take you right out of the meeting.

Use an observation sheet with categories down the left-hand side and group member's names along the top:

| Observation sheet | | | | Date: | | | | Time: | |
|---|---|---|---|---|---|---|---|---|---|
| Names | John | Eric | Mike | Tom | Anne | Sheila | David | Joan | Total |
| Proposing | II | ⊬⊬ I | ⊬⊬ | | I | | I | I | 16 |
| Giving information | I | IIII | ⊬⊬ III | I | II | II | I | I | 20 |
| Seeking information | III | I | ⊬⊬ I | III | | | | | |
| . . . and so on . . . | | | | | | | | | |

*Table A17.2*

Practise on two or four behaviours and two or four people until you get the hang of it. Try logging Mike and Eric on 'proposing', 'giving information', 'seeking information', and 'supporting/building'. High contributors do a lot of proposing and giving information but very little information seeking.

Some generalizations are that groups do a lot of giving—information, proposals, etc. but very little seeking—information, understanding, etc. 'Building' is a rare behaviour and 'summarizing' all too rare. 'Defending/ attacking' creates similar responses in others and a sort of escalation or spiral occurs.

From your observations over a number of meetings and 15-minute periods you should be able to answer some of the following:

—Do people fall into stereotyped roles? For example, just as there are habitual low contributors are there chronic proposers who do no suporting and consenters who do no disagreeing?

—Is there a balance of behaviours in the group? For example, people may fall into particular roles, but if these complement each other then the group may function well. Unless somebody *is* doing the summarizing, testing understanding, supporting, etc., several vital functions will be missing.

—How could this group work better? For example, does everybody feel O.K. about their roles, levels of contribution, and rewards from this group?; does the group make good decisions without undue wasting of time?

Again, the group could benefit from having your observations fed back to them, but most groups are not used to such self-scrutiny and will tend to reject you, the data, or both. Caution is recommended.

**Part 3**

You can dispense with some of the caution and be as experimental as you like with your own behaviour. After all this observation you will have put together some ideas about the way *you* behave in groups. Spend some time now summarizing these.

*Step 1*

What characteristics have you noticed in yourself?

—Are you a medium, low, or high contributor?

—Are you a proposer, a builder, or what?

—How much seeking behaviour do you practise?

—What happened the last time you were in a defending/attacking position?

—How often do you test your understanding of other people's ideas?

*Step 2*

Choose some of the behaviours you'd like to practise more often; some you'd like to cut back on.

*Step 3*

At the next meeting you attend, experiment by using one new behaviour. If you're trying to lessen a behaviour, try cutting it out altogether.

*Step 4*

Observe carefully what effect you're having. You may be able to elicit feedback from people's behaviour towards you in the meeting or by conversations afterwards.

*Step 5*

If you're stuck for behaviours to try, remember that seeking information, building, summarizing, and testing understanding are often low in groups. Here are some suggested actions.

At the next meeting try one of the following:

—Do nothing but ask questions.

—Never ask a question.

—Do not agree or disagree with anything.

—Each time you're not absolutely sure what another person means, ask him for clarification.

—If you're a high contributor normally—say nothing: if you're normally low—aim to say more than anyone else.

FOLLOW-UP

There will always be meetings in which you can observe and experiment. One thing we promise you, if you use these ideas you will never look at a meeting in the same way again. You will notice things that passed you by before.

If you'd like to read more about groups and group behaviour Edgar Schein's two little books are exceptionally good: *Organisational Psychology* (2nd edn.) (Prentice Hall, 1970), particularly chapter 5; *Process Consultation: its Role in Organisation Development* (Addison-Wesley, 1969), particularly chapters 3 and 8. The second book spends much time on the observer's role and how to use the data gathered. The categories used in this activity are taken from Neil Rackham's work. If you want to read more about this and see what other categories there are and what you can do with them see: *Developing Interactive Skills* edited by Neil Rackham, Peter Honey, and Michael Colbert (Wellens Publishing, 1971) and, more recently, *Behaviour Analysis in Training* by Neil Rackham and Terry Morgan (McGraw-Hill, 1977).

# Activity 18
## Interpreting yourself and others

LEARNING AREAS: SOCIAL SKILLS: Self-knowledge: Analytical skills

The way you behave towards other people, and your success and failure in achieving things with and through other people, depends very much on the extent to which you see them as they see themselves, and you see yourself as they see you.

Every action you take to influence another person is based on a complex set of conscious or unconscious assumptions about the meaning they will attach to your action and the way in which they will respond to it.

Part 1 of this activity is designed to help you become aware of some of the ways you see other people and yourself.

Part 2 suggests that you check this out in some way to see how your perceptions coincide with those of others.

**Activity. Part 1**

*Step 1*

In the boxes in column 1 of Fig. A18.2 write the names of five people with whom you interact frequently in the work context, about things that are important to your work and your organization's functioning.

*Step 2*

In columns 2 and 3 are further boxes, joined in pairs by horizontal lines. These lines represent dimensions on which people might differ (e.g., aggressive–meek, clever–stupid, honest–devious, etc.) in your mind. Each dimension is joined to two of the name boxes in column 1. Take each 'dimension' in turn and look at the names of the people in the two boxes. Think of a way in which these two people seem different to you, and a pair of words, like quick–slow, funny–serious, reliable–unreliable, to describe that difference. Put one word in the box at each end of the dimension. It does not matter which end you put the words. Do this 10 times, once for each of the dimensions. Try to make sure you find a different dimension each time. It does not matter if you do not account for all, or even the main

155

differences between the two people each time, as long as you get one aspect of it. The idea is to find out the ways in which you classify people.

*Step 3*

Treating each dimension as a scale, put a cross on it where you think you are, and mark it with your initials. (See Fig. A18.1.)

*Figure A18.1*

Treat the dimension as a scale from extreme to extreme—e.g., complete reliability to complete unreliability, even if the people who led you to think of it in the first place are not at the extremes.

**Part 2**

Part 1 should have given you food for thought about yourself in relation to those with whom you work. You can get more from it. Here are some possibilities:

(a)  Decide what you would *like* to be like by ticking the dimensions where you would like to be.

(b)  Try *being* different. If you can do so, is it what you really want?

(c)  Choose one of the 'five'; mark where you think he is on each dimension, and show it to him, getting his reaction to where you put him and yourself.

(d)  Do the exercise with one or more of the others, sharing and discussing your conclusions.

(e)  As you go about your normal activities, see if you can find ways of checking whether you see others as they see themselves, and whether they see you as you see yourself.

FOLLOW-UP

You will get much more out of this if you involve yourself in getting other people's views. 'Where to go from here' is to simply develop the habit and skill of checking on your perceptions of others, and on how you come across to them.

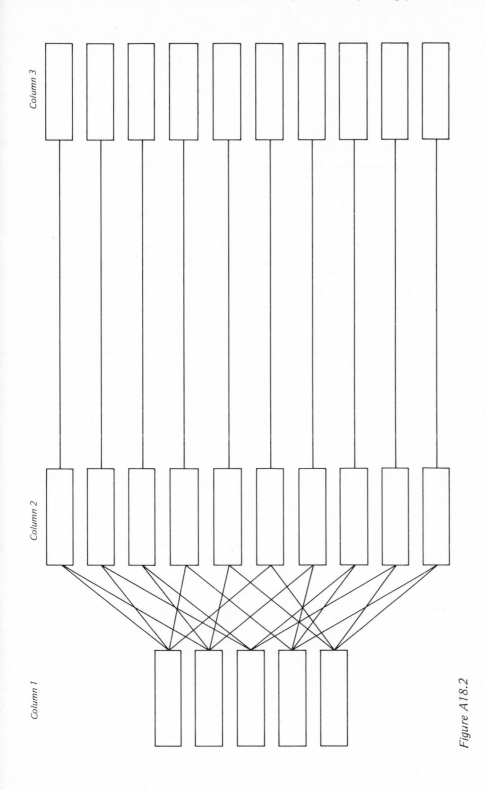

Figure A18.2

# Activity 19
## Counselling style inventory

LEARNING AREAS: SOCIAL SKILLS: Sensitivity to events: Self-knowledge

Much of a manager's time with his subordinates is spent in a listening, receiving posture. The ideal manager is a helper who provides personal support for his staff. Leonard Sayles calls this function 'responsiveness' and notes that if a manager is accessible to his staff they will often come just to have him listen.[1] Listening is a key managerial skill and one of the aspects which subordinates value most.

In the hectic environment of the work world, there is also the need for action. A manager achieves results through other people working well and some of his most important actions concern the motivation of subordinates. This is rarely a simple 'carrot and stick' exercise, but a complex process requiring a detailed knowledge of the individual needs of subordinates, and considerable helping skills. Help is not always helpful, however, as all those who have been helped, advised, and put right will know. Deciding what is helpful in a given situation is a skill in itself.

We'll call this listening and helping activity 'counselling'. The following activity will help you to analyse your counselling style.

Activity

Five short paragraphs depict statements from people who might be your subordinates, and five sets of five responses to the statements. You are to choose the response which you feel you would most likely make. Be honest with yourself—there are no simple 'right answers'—and you have everything to gain from an honest analysis of your behaviour.

When you have read Situation A turn to the five responses and choose one. Then turn back and read Situation B, and so on.

158

SITUATION A

*Man, aged 35 years*

'I have a lot of ambition. Every job I've had I've been successful at, and I intend to be successful here even if it means walking over a few people to do so. I'm going to prove myself and really go places.'

SITUATION B

*Woman, aged 26 years*

'Two years at business school have really equipped me to be a professional manager. Competing with men there has convinced me that women who get as far as I have are more than a match for most men. If this organization wants to keep me they'll have to fit in with my own career progression.'

SITUATION C

*Man, aged 44*

'I used to be very ambitious but, as I've got older, success is not so important to me. I may not have been a success with the company, but I've put all my real effort into my family. I'm a very happy family man.'

SITUATION D

*Woman, aged 41*

'When I moved to this town I thought I'd make lots of new friends. Being single and living alone I've always had quite a social life . . .. But, it doesn't seem to happen somehow . . . the work is fine, but people here aren't interested in socializing much. I think it must be me . . . I'm getting more closed up and into myself . . ..'

SITUATION E

*Man, aged 32*

'I'm telling you, Lewis has really got his knife into me. I got the blame for the whole of the Brown and Williamson affair and there were eight of us involved. Now he's trying to insinuate I'm falling down on the job. I had a good name in this office until he came here—he just doesn't like me and he's determined to do me down.'

| SITUATION A |    Choose *one* of the following responses:

1. 'You feel you are a very ambitious man, is that right?'

2. 'Why do you think you have such strong needs for success?'

3. 'That's good. You should soon get to the top with that attitude. Let me know if I can help you in any way.'

4. 'It seems to me that your needs for success are so strong that they outweigh your needs to be popular.'

5. 'It will make you very unpopular here if you maintain that attitude, that's not how we do things here at all.'

| SITUATION B |    Choose *one* of the following responses:

1. 'A business school education is a great asset, but if you ask me it doesn't make you a good manager. You have to learn that the hard way.'

2. 'What difficulties do you foresee in being female in this organization?'

3. 'I'm sure you're right. We are really in need of people with your skills and drive. Let's get together next week and I'll help you plan out how you can get the experience you want in this department in the shortest possible time.'

4. 'If I'm hearing you correctly, you feel that you are well equipped as a professional manager and you expect the organization to respect this?'

5. 'It appears to me that you have some worries about being accorded the status you think you deserve?'

| SITUATION C |    Choose *one* of the following responses:

1. 'That sounds like a very sensible attitude, after all, very few people get to the top. Is there any help I can give you in this?'

2. Yes, you reached the point where you decided to switch goals—from your career to your family—but you feel perhaps that something is missing?'

3. 'You're absolutely right. A man's a fool to keep struggling when nobody cares a damn. You did the right thing and I'd do the same in your position.'

4. 'As you have got older you find more and more satisfaction with your family.'

5. 'Why do you feel that you weren't a success with the company? What do you mean by success?'

SITUATION D    Choose *one* of the following responses:

1. 'Can you tell me more about how you go about making friends. Have you made any efforts recently to meet people?'

2. 'Living alone is O.K. if you have lots of friends, but without them it's very lonely—is that what you're saying?'

3. 'It looks as though you may be really worried about the future, perhaps you've lived alone for so long that you've dropped out of the habit of getting close to people?'

4. 'That sounds really sad, to be lonely and without friends. What you've got to do is get out and about and make some. . .. If I were you I'd get started straight away.'

5. 'Well, let's see . . . there are lots of ways in which you could get involved with the staff social club. Next month there's the annual outing and I could get you on the organizing team, how would you like that?'

SITUATION E    Choose *one* of the following responses:

1. 'You are getting paranoic feelings about Lewis, could it be that you are working out your frustrations at not getting the job you both applied for?'

2. 'You're right, he can really be a mean so-and-so when he chooses, but I wouldn't go about it with your attitude.'

3. 'Are there any other occasions when he's tried to show you up in a poor light?'

4. 'If I understand you correctly; you feel persecuted by Lewis and think that he intends to wreck your reputation?'

5. 'Right, you need to protect yourself from situations like this. Do you know that the union is becoming very strong among our grades, in fact, I've got some application forms here, I'll help you fill them out.'

SCORING

In the grid below, the situations are listed on the left-hand side and the responses (1 to 5) fall into the five categories E, I, S, P, U along the top.

Look at the response you selected for each situation and note which letter it falls under. For example, if you chose response 3 to Situation A then you note one 'S'. Do this for all five situations.

RESPONSES

| | | E | I | S | P | U |
|---|---|---|---|---|---|---|
| S I T U A T I O N S | A | 5 | 4 | 3 | 2 | 1 |
| | B | 1 | 5 | 3 | 2 | 4 |
| | C | 3 | 2 | 1 | 5 | 4 |
| | D | 4 | 3 | 5 | 1 | 2 |
| | E | 2 | 1 | 5 | 3 | 4 |

*Table A19.1*

You should now have a score for all five types of responses, e.g., how many E's did you score? how many I's? and so on, for example:

*Responses*

| | |
|---|---|
| E | 2 |
| I | 1 |
| S | 2 |
| P | — |
| U | — |
| | 5 |

DISCUSSION

This exercise is based on the work of Carl Rogers who developed these five response categories[2] from studies done on face-to-face communication. These categories accounted for 80 per cent of all messages sent between people and generally speaking are used as follows:

E—used most
I—used next most
S—used third most
P—fourth most
U—used least

The categories are as follows:

| | |
|---|---|
| E—Evaluative response | —making judgements. |
| I—Interpretative response | —'reading between the lines', making hunches. |
| S—Supportive response | —agreeing, backing up, offering psychological and actual support. |
| P—Probing response | —questioning, asking for more, often deeper, information. |
| U—Understanding response | —understanding is used in a rather special way—it refers to a non-directive, non-evaluative response which reflects back to the speaker what he/she said. |

The categories themselves are neither good nor bad. They are more or less appropriate in particular situations.

*What is important* is that:

**1.** We tend to have habitual, fixed ways of responding therefore we over-use some categories and under-use others.
Which categories do you over-use?
Which categories do you under-use?

**2.** People tend to pigeonhole us—Rogers says that if we use any one response for 40 per cent or more of the time, then *we are always seen as behaving like that.*
Did you score two E's, I's, S's, P's, or U's?

If so, you may be seen as being this sort of person. If you scored three or four for one type of response, then you are likely to be using this sort of response consistently. Other people almost certainly have this image of you.
Don't forget that there is no right way of behaving for all situations. The purpose of this activity is to highlight your counselling style and illustrate some alternative.

FOLLOW-UP

Interpersonal behaviour is far too complex to capture on a few sheets of two-dimensional paper. The activity is valid if you think it has something to say to you. If you want to look at Carl Rogers's ideas in more detail—go to his *Client-Centred Therapy* mentioned in the references or to his *On Becoming a Person* (Constable, 1971).

More specifically on counselling, there is a shortage of good simple texts, *Basic Counselling* by John Shaw (Vernon Scott Associates, 1973) is good but may be difficult to get. *The Helping Relationship: Process and Skills* by Lawrence Brammer (Prentice Hall, 1971) is a wider, more scholarly work, but very good value.

A good way of follow-up—as with all managerial skills—is to practise, as often as you can in real situations. Using the framework in this activity you can experiment with new types of responses—try to do more probing or reflecting back. If you are habitually non-directive, be more supportive and evaluative at times.

## REFERENCES

1. Sayles, L., *Managerial Behaviour*, McGraw-Hill, 1964, pp. 149–153.
2. Rogers, C. R., *Client-Centred Therapy*, Houghton Mifflin, 1951.

# Activity 20
## Getting to know you

LEARNING AREAS: SOCIAL SKILLS: Self-knowledge

To get to know somebody well, we have to do more than talk about trivial things. We have to reveal significant aspects of ourselves and of our lives; in turn, the other person is likely to reveal something of him or herself. This mutual process of exchanging personal information leads to better understanding and acceptance of each other.

Everyday social norms, and natural reticence, usually prevent us from talking openly with strangers—even with fairly close acquaintances. This activity is therefore designed in such a way that personal open exchanges are legitimized. It can be used in any situation where you want to get to know somebody else reasonably well, reasonably quickly. At the same time you will find the process of sharing and receiving personal information will increase your level of self-understanding.

*Activity*

If you are carrying out a self-development programme with a partner (see chapter 7), this activity is a good way to get started.

Before commencing the activity make sure that each of you *wants* to get to know the other better.

Find a place where you won't be disturbed and set aside at least an hour.

*Instructions*

Read these instructions carefully before looking at Table A20.1.

You will find a number of incomplete statements. Starting with the first, one of you should complete the statement by telling your partner as much or as little as you want. Your partner can respond to what you say in any way he likes. In turn the partner should complete the statement and you can respond to him in any way you wish. When this process is complete, move on to statement 2, and so on.

Don't look ahead at the other statements—concentrate only on the one being discussed.

Be as revealing as you like—it is entirely up to each person to decide how much to say.

Stop this activity whenever either one of you wishes to do so.

## WHEN YOU ARE READY, BEGIN:

1. My name is . . .

2. My job is . . .

3. My age is . . .

4. I live . . .

5. I was born in . . .

6. My previous jobs included . . .

7. Things I like best about this job are . . .

8. Things I like least about this job are . . .

9. My marital status is . . .

10. Children . . .

11. My parents . . .

12. My friends . . .

13. My hobbies/spare-time activities . . .

14. When I get to work . . .

15. When I leave work . . .

16. At this very minute, I feel . . .

17. Ideally, this time next year . . .

18. In the long term, my ambition . . .

19. The trouble with this organization is . . .

20. My idea of an ideal holiday would be . . .

*Table A20.1.  The statements*

21. Things that I find very difficult . . .

22. If the worst comes to the worst in 12 months time . . .

23. The sort of things I worry about . . .

24. What this country needs . . .

25. My religious beliefs . . .

26. My secret fears . . .

27. My feelings about you . . .

28. My feelings about myself are . . .

*Table A20.1* (Continued)

## FOLLOW-UP

When you have finished this activity, reflect on it.

How did you feel?

How open and revealing were you?

Were you more open about some types of issue rather than others?

# Activity 21
## Relaxation

When man first evolved, he was constantly faced with threats in the form of dangerous animals, warring bands, and so on. His reaction to these threats was to get rid of them—either directly by fighting them, or indirectly by fleeing from them.

To help with these reactions the human body (like that of animals) prepared itself in various ways. These include an increased rate of breathing, a raised blood pressure, faster heart beats, greater flow of blood to muscles, and a number of other complex and interrelated physiological responses.

Today's manager, seldom faced with danger from wild beasts, yet finds himself in a number of threatening situations. In the course of his job he will become involved in deals, with conflicts, in meeting difficult deadlines, in making decisions with inadequate information. He will negotiate, confront, take risks. Often—increasingly so these days—his own job security may seem to be in considerable doubt.

Although the types of stressful situation that the manager faces are very different from those of his ancestors, his body's response is identical. In these situations there are marked increases in his pulse rate, blood pressure, breathing, etc.

Unfortunately, these body responses—while excellent for preparing us either to fight a wild beast or to run as fast as possible—don't help us to cope with managerial problems. Furthermore, as we usually don't actually fight or run, all the physiological changes have to be channelled into other effects.

Some of these, particularly in the short term, can be seen as displaced fight or flight behaviour. Shouting or snapping irritably is a form of flight. If we are frightened of our boss, we may 'fight' someone with less power to retaliate, such as a subordinate, wife, or child. Flight behaviour can be seen in numerous forms, including never-ending attempts to change jobs, day-dreaming, putting vast energies into tackling other problems (which are in fact much easier, even trivial), and headaches and other elusive but painful symptoms that give us the socially acceptable escape route of being 'off colour', going home early, or staying home ill.

In the longer term, the body's responses to stressful and threatening situations, are to gradually build up, with very real and serious consequences, the conditions that lead to heart attacks, strokes, ulcers, colitis.

One way of coping with the more immediate physical symptoms of stress is by taking tranquillizers. However, these can hardly be recommended as a long-term solution; what is needed is an internal method of coping with stress reactions.

In recent years a number of such internal methods have grown in popularity. These are often associated with specific cults, philosophies, or religions. Yoga is a well-known approach; transcendental meditation is another.

The activity suggested here is not associated with any particular cult or belief system, but is based on a synthesis of the common elements of a number of approaches to relaxation. More than with most of the activities in this book, you need to repeat this activity over a longish period of time for it to work at its best.

**Activity**

*Step 1*

Find a quiet place where you can sit down comfortably. It is important to be fairly straight and upright. Although some people like to sit cross-legged on the floor, this is not essential and you may be more comfortable in a chair. In this case sit with both feet on the ground, back straight, head up. Don't be *too* comfortable—you mustn't fall asleep.

*Step 2*

When you are comfortable, close your eyes and then consciously relax all your muscles, starting at the top of your head and moving down through your body to the tips of your toes. If you have difficulty in doing this, tell yourself that you are becoming more and more relaxed, that you are going deeper . . . and deeper . . . and deeper. It is often helpful to imagine yourself going down, in a lift; on an escalator; in warm water; to the bottom of the sea.

*Step 3*

Breathe through your nose, and listen to your own breathing. As you become more relaxed you will notice your breathing become slower, shallower, and more restful. Notice that at the bottom of each breath (i.e., after breathing out) there is a pause before you begin to breath again.

*Step 4*

When you have noticed these pauses, start counting backwards from ten to one. Count thus: breathe out: TEN: breathe in: breathe out: NINE: breathe in: breathe out: EIGHT: etc. Count in this way from ten down to one, than back up from one to ten, down from ten to one, and so on.

*Step 5*

Stray thoughts may come into your head while you are breathing/counting. Don't worry about this; just let the thought come, don't dwell on it, let it go. Then go back to TEN and start counting again. Don't worry if you never reach ONE, especially in the early days.

Step 6

Continue breathing/counting in this way for 15 to 20 minutes (although 10 minutes may be easier to start with) at least once a day; twice is better. Keep a watch or clock handy, and check if you wish (otherwise keep your eyes closed). When you finish, remain sitting quietly for a few minutes, then stand up slowly.

FOLLOW-UP

This activity is one that should be incorporated into your life style to be of maximum benefit.

Once you have mastered this basic relaxation technique, you might like to carry it a stage farther. One fascinating book that contains a number of more advanced methods is *Passages* by Marianne Anderson and Louis Savary (Turnstone Books, 1974).

Three other good books on the effects of stress, the need to relax, and methods of relaxation are: *The Relaxation Response* by Herbert Benson (Collins, 1976); *Stress: How to Stop Your Mind Killing Your Body* by Walter McQuade and Ann Aikman (Hutchison, 1976); *Relax* by Jane Madders (BBC Publications, 1973).

# **Activity 22**
## Fitness

There is a steadily growing recognition of the essential link between physical fitness, on the one hand, and mental alertness, high morale, motivation, and general effectiveness on the other.

In this activity we simply stress the importance of this aspect of self-development, and make one or two suggestions about the sources of further guidance. For example, many local authorities run 'keep fit' programmes; some colleges put on activities specifically designed for managers and businessmen; there are also many books on the subject.

You should find a regime of regular exercise which suits you—your personality, life style, age, present level of fitness, and so on—and build it into your work and life. This will not only make you feel physically better, it will have a payoff in all areas of your work—particularly where you are in stressful, demanding situations. To be a successful manager, you can't afford not to be fit!

Three books can be recommended: *The New Aerobics* by K. H. Cooper (Bantam Books, 1970) (This book has been reprinted 18 times!); *Don't Just Sit There* (BBC Publications, 1973); *Fit for Life* by H. B. Wright, G. Pincherle, and A. Murray (Evans Brothers, 1968).

# Activity 23
## Managing your feelings

LEARNING AREAS: SOCIAL SKILLS: Emotional resilience: Self-knowledge

One of the factors which contribute to emotional resilience is awareness of one's own feelings. This awareness is a requirement for the control and management of feelings. We do not want to overstress the controlling aspect. The manager who always maintains a stiff upper lip, in classical British tradition, is bottling up natural feelings. He may not even fully realize this. One day the dam may burst in some uncontrolled way, leading perhaps to a nervous breakdown or psychosomatic illness.

Open expression of feelings is not only beneficial to the individual, but also leads to more open interpersonal relationships. This must be qualified. If there is a strong norm in your organization that open expression of feelings is somehow taboo, your colleagues may be surprised or even shocked to find you breaking this rule.

We express feelings by what we say, but much more significant factors are the way we say it, and non-verbal cues such as facial expression, gesture, and posture.

The main purpose of this activity is to develop awareness of your feelings so that a choice can be made about their expression. Bottling up or free expression are alternative ways of handling feelings, both appropriate in particular situations. If you bottle feelings up, you'll have to express them somehow, somewhere, but the successful manager 'manages' this expression.

The activity is designed to give you practice at becoming aware of, and expressing your feelings—and at identifying feelings that are being expressed by someone else.

### The activity

Steps 1 and 2 of the activity should be done with a partner, although it is possible to do Step 1 on your own, using a tape recorder. If you do so, follow the instructions, record your voice, and listen to a play-back. Even with a partner, you will derive extra benefit from using a tape recorder.

172

Interpret the word 'partner' liberally—it can be a colleague, spouse, or friend, or even a small group of four or five persons.

The first step focuses on the expression of feelings through the *way we speak*, as opposed to *what we say*.

Copy out this list of feelings onto small cards or pieces of paper—one feeling per piece.

| | |
|---|---|
| Excited | Patronizing |
| Angry | Depressed |
| Sarcastic | Bored |
| Happy | Tired |
| Affectionate | Enthusiastic |
| Disliking | Frightened |
| Threatened | Curious |
| Superior | Preoccupied |
| Cautious | Interested |

Shuffle the cards/papers, and select one at random. Imagine that your partner has just said or done something that evokes in you the feeling on the card. Get into the mood of that feeling and then say to him, in a way that demonstrates that feeling, the following:

'Well now there are lots of implications in this.'

Your partner has to guess what emotion or feeling you are trying to convey. If he's wrong, try again.

Take it in turns to express and guess feelings.

Discuss the experience together. Were there some feelings that you found relatively easy or difficult to express? If so, why do you think this was?

Were you surprised at the level of accuracy or inaccuracy of your partner's ability to perceive your emotion? Or at your own ability to judge his? What are the implications of your answers?

This step deals with the non-verbal expression of feelings, such as by facial expression, gesture, body posture, etc.

The procedure is the same as in Step 1, except that instead of expressing feelings through the sentence 'Well now there are lots of implications in this', you may do so in any way you wish *provided that you do not speak*.

Again, take turns and then discuss.

*Step 3*

This step moves back into everyday activities. It requires you to examine the feelings you experience from time to time, to identify how you *think* you expressed them, and to check out this belief with other people concerned.

To help with this, use the 'feelings log', Table A23.1. In column 1, write down how you felt on each particular occasion. Then try to think why you felt that way, and note that briefly in column 2.

It is worth looking out for a phenomenon that many managers experience without being aware of it. Having noted how you felt, try to identify *what you were feeling just before*—even though this preliminary feeling may have lasted for a very short time.

| 1 | 2 | 3 | 4 | 5 |
|---|---|---|---|---|
| *Your feelings at a particular time* | *What caused these feelings?* | *Did you express your feelings?* | *If not, why not? If so, how did you express them?* | *Check with others. How did they think you were feeling? Why?* |
| | | | | |

*Table A23.1*

When an event triggers off a particular feeling we often find this unacceptable and switch to another emotion. As was mentioned earlier, anger is often preceded by a brief feeling of threat, anger being a defence against that threat. This insight is helpful in controlling behaviour and in responding more productively to situations. So, if you are able to identify short feelings-links, note these down.

In column 3, answer yes or no to the question 'Did you express your feelings?'. If your answer is no, try to explain why not in column 4. If the answer is yes, describe in column 4 how you think you expressed them.

Finally, use column 5 to check out with the other people involved in the situation whether or not they correctly perceived your feelings. Ask them what *they* thought you were feeling, and why. Compare this with your own perceptions of your feelings, and the way in which you did or did not express them.

After a number of entries in the feelings log, look for patterns or repeating themes. Do certain types of events lead to certain feelings? What different causes lead to a particular feeling? Which feelings do you express, which do you not? Why? When do you express feelings? When don't you? To whom do you express them? To whom don't you? Do people sense some of your feelings, but not others? Are some people more accurate in their perception of your feelings than others?

# Activity 24
## Stability zones

LEARNING AREAS: EMOTIONAL RESILIENCE

Reaching the limits of 'emotional resilience' is often experienced as loss of control, of ability to cope with the demands made and the changes going on around an individual. Alvin Toffler in his book[1] suggested that we can all cope with an enormous amount of change, pressure, complexity, and confusion, provided that at least one area of our lives or ourselves is relatively stable. This 'stability zone' serves as a mental retreat and anchor which allows us to cope with change and complexity in other areas.

The main kinds of stability zone are related to IDEAS, PLACES, THINGS, PEOPLE, and ORGANIZATIONS. Working out where *your* stability zones are or could be, and planning to cultivate them, may help you develop your capacity to cope with pressures in other areas.

IDEAS may take the form of a deeply felt religious belief, or a strong commitment to a philosophy, political ideology, or cause. It may take the form of a strong interest in an area of professional activity and its underlying theory.

PLACES mean geographical places: large scale (like your country), or small scale (like your street or your office). Places as stability zones are often 'home', where one grew up or has spent considerable time, and which has a comforting familiarity about it.

People whose stability zones are places will always feel a little strange anywhere else and take comfort from the knowledge that they can return to home base. Managerial careers often demand that one becomes cosmopolitan—living away from 'home' and moving on every few years. Some learn to do without a stability zone, others find ways of keeping some geographical roots alive.

THINGS as stability zones take the form of favourite, familiar, comforting possessions. It may be clothes, like that old jacket or pair of shoes, or it may be family heirlooms. It may be items from childhood or the paraphernalia of a hobby. It may be houses (obviously related to PLACES) or books (related to IDEAS). It is often motor cars.

176

PEOPLE means valued and enduring relationships with others. Very often family will be the source of PEOPLE stability zones but it may also be long-standing friends and colleagues.

ORGANIZATIONS as stability zones may be the work organization, a professional body or institute, a club, or any other form of organization to which one belongs and with which one 'identifies'.

Stability zones may overlap, for example 'home' has elements of place, people, and things.

One can cope with considerable change and instability in many of these areas at once, provided one has a stable base in at least one. So, for example, the person centred around an idea, belief, or cause may be able to lead a nomadic life with no enduring possessions, getting through organizations and spouses at great speed.

Activity

Work through the following questions, on paper, making notes in answer to them. They are intended to help you think about your stability zones, whether they do and will serve you well, whether you should deliberately cultivate them.

*Step 1. What are YOUR stability zones?*

Write down your thoughts, think through the five areas of ideas, places, things, people, and organizations. Ask yourself what you would change and what you would not—your car, your organizations, your spouse, your possessions, your house.

*Step 2. How stable are your stability zones?*

Are your basic ideas and beliefs sound? Can you count on staying in your 'places' and on your places staying the same? Do your possessions continue to satisfy? Will they last, or eventually wear out? Can you count on the people you rely on to stay around? Can you count on the organizations you want to belong to wanting you to belong to them?

*Step 3. Will your stability zones serve you in the future?*

Things change with the passing of time. Objects wear out, houses become too big or too small, children grow up and leave home, organizations and places change, other people have their own lives to follow, ideas are sometimes found wanting or deficient, or reach their limits. Some activities, like sport, become more difficult with age, and everyone retires some time, unless they drop dead first!

*Step 4.  Can you influence the existence of your stability zones?*

Are the ideas, places, things, people, and organizations that you depend on to any extent under your control?

*Step 5.  Do you invest enough in your stability zones?*

Do you work on developing your ideas, look after and maintain your possessions, care for the people that are important to you?

*Step 6.  How compatible are your stability zones with your main, particularly your work, activities?*

*Step 7.  Are there any changes you want to make in your stability zones, and how you use and maintain them?*

Write yourself an action plan BY WRITING A LETTER TO YOURSELF AS YOU HOPE YOU WILL BE IN SIX MONTHS TIME.

## FOLLOW-UP

You can get further useful ideas about coping with stress by reading the book (reference 1) and from which the idea of 'stability zones' is taken. You may also find *Managerial Stress* edited by D. Gowler and K. Legge (Gower Press, 1975) a useful source of ideas.

## REFERENCES

1.  Toffler, A., *Future Shock*, Pan Books, 1970.

# Activity 25
## Who's the boss?

LEARNING AREAS: PROACTIVITY: Analytical skills: Social skills

Whatever your level of management you probably have the right to be boss of at least one group of other managers who help you to make important decisions.

In complex, interdependent social systems decisions are very rarely ours to take alone. Just as management has long since lost the right to decide unilaterally (without reference to employees) so most of us must consult and communicate to be able to decide on important issues.

Decisions about changes, decisions on problems, decisions about where to go and what to do are all made and often negotiated with those who are most concerned with the particular decision.

But, who is really the 'boss' on important decisions that affect your life? It should be you and you should be able to choose the team to help you make good decisions and not hold you back. Some people will give as well as take from you; others will only take; their impact is largely destructive. The former cause you to grow and strengthen from your interaction with them; the latter weaken you.

This activity offers you an opportunity to select managers, to establish yourself as the boss over them, perhaps even to remove those whose influence is not helpful, even harmful.

Activity

*Step 1*

Choose a decision which has to be made—now or in the near future. Don't choose a decision which has already been taken—the more 'live' the issue the better.

The decision should not be a simple choice between clear alternatives, but a complex matter involving others and their feelings and relationships, and affecting a number of areas of your life.

Choosing a new car would not be a very good example to choose; changing your job or moving house would be. It may be one of your life's goals that you want to change, or some aspect of the way you've been living. Perhaps a major decision affecting your children—their education, upbringing, or future.

*Step 2*

Thinking of this decision and using the 'boardroom' diagram (Fig. A25.1) write in the name of the 'managers' who have a say in the making of this decision. Six to twelve is a good number. Put their initials on the chairs round the table.

*Figure A25.1*

*Step 3*

Next to each of the 'managers' jot down some notes on the advice he or she would give on this decision.

*Step 4*

Take a good look at this advice. Ask yourself of each manager in turn:

    —Whose interest does she/he have at heart in making points, hers/his or yours?

    —Is she/he interested in getting a good decision or not?

    —How biased is she/he?

*Step 5*

If you are the boss you take the decisions. You also have a say in who sits on the management team, although you can't remove people just because you don't like them. You need to distinguish between liking a person and concern for a good decision—he has a right to be there even if you don't like his advice.

Take a look at your management team:

(a)  Are you really the boss?

(b)  Are there any managers who shouldn't be there?

(c)  Have you got enough advice of the right kind? Could you use a new manager? Perhaps to replace one of your less useful ones?

# Activity 26
## Practising change

LEARNING AREAS: PROACTIVITY: Sensitivity to events: Emotional resilience

It is commonplace to talk about the accelerating rate of change in society. More than in any previously recorded age, we have to learn continuously, to cope and keep up. No one grows old and dies in the world in which he was born, and the stresses and demands placed upon us help to account for the explosion of the so-called 'helping professions'. Still the growth in numbers of teachers, social workers, and medical staff fails to cope with the by-products of change. Voluntary associations find their resources over-stretched and the consumption of anti-depressant drugs speaks for itself.

Change creates problems for management. A large part of management is the efficient administration and deployment of resources via systems, pro-cedures, and routines. This 'determined' part of a manager's job is relatively easy to specify and train for. The other part, the unpredictable 'discretion-ary' element, can't be programmed. As change increases so does the discretionary portion of a manager's work. Moreover, this is usually the critical portion, the part where the difference between right and wrong decisions can be measured on the balance sheet.

To cope with his job—and to cope with himself—every manager needs to become familiar with the effects of change on himself and on other people. This does not imply that every manager spends all his time implementing change. On many occasions he will resist change and seek to minimize its effects. He is, however, responsible for the work of other people and therefore for the effects of change on this work. He needs to be intimately concerned with the planning of change and the anticipation of its effects.

This activity contains a number of short experiments which call for risk taking to experience and learn about the effects of change. The objective is to practise change on yourself. What you learn as a result of the risks you take and the changes you make will prepare you for changes imposed on you and over which you have no control. It will also prepare you for planning the implementation of change with your staff—you will learn how it feels, what reactions to expect, and how to cope with them.

182

A word about risk taking. A recent theory of human change and development suggests that we learn by making *investments* of a modest kind in
certain new behaviours. These new behaviours are chosen on the basis of
what we know of the world (COGNITIONS) and what we know of ourselves
(SENSE OF IDENTITY). We learn from the feedback which we get from
these investments—good or bad, pleasant or unpleasant. If we can accept
even negative feedback then our cognitions and identity and perceptions are
enhanced.[1] Learning always involves risk—we are moving from what we
know and are familiar with to what we don't know and are unsure of. The
more deep and fundamental the learning, the more risk is involved. Hence
'bad' or 'negative' feedback is important—often more important than 'good'
feedback, if only because we often choose to ignore it.

The following activities call for moderate risks from you. They also offer the
opportunity of learning about yourself and others. Start with these and if
you want to go further, design some of your own risk taking and change
situations.

*Activities*

*Experiment 1: Eating a new food*

The next time you go to a restaurant, or even the canteen if the menu is
varied enough, eat a new dish which you haven't tried before.

| | |
|---|---|
| *Before eating* | —What are your expectations about the experience you are about to have? |
| | —Is it going to be pleasant or unpleasant, exciting or stressful? |
| | —What are you feelings as you approach the food? |
| *While eating* | —Concentrate solely on eating, especially the first mouthful. Chew slowly, don't talk, and don't be distracted from the food. |
| *After eating* | —How does this compare with your normal approach to food? |
| | —How much of a risk did you take? |
| | —What did you gain as a result of your investment? |
| | —What did you learn about changing to the unfamiliar? |

*Experiment 2: Changing your surroundings*

Choose a room where you spend a considerable part of your time. If you
have an office then this would probably be the best, but if not, try a room at

home. The experiment involves rearranging the furniture. You can also take down pictures and remove decorations, or put some up if your room is rather bare.

| | |
|---|---|
| *Before rearranging* | —Where else could the major pieces of furniture go? |
| | —What other layout is possible? |
| | —What alterations could be made to the decorations? |
| *Rearranging* | —Note carefully where you are putting things in your new arrangement. |
| *After rearranging* | —How comfortable do you feel now? (Allow at least a few hours before changing again.) |
| | —What effect does the new layout have on your behaviour? What are you doing differently? |
| | —How do other people react to your new layout? (Try and arrange for as many as possible to view and comment on the change.) |
| | —What have you learned about the effects of physical surroundings? |
| | —What have you learned about change and its effects on behaviour? |

If you got something out of this investment, try another layout or rearrangement.

How long is it since you looked at the fixtures and fittings in your behaviour as a manager and considered a spring-clean and rearrangement?

*Experiment 3: Changing your image*

Obviously there are many, many ways in which you can do this. For the purpose of this experiment, let's choose three areas of yourself which the outside world has most contact with. These are:

Your style of dress;
Your style of writing;
Your style of greeting.

'Impression management' is a jargon-term for personal public relations. What we suggest here is that you try a few changes in these three areas and watch for the results.

| | |
|---|---|
| *Dress* | Choose some change or other. Leave your tie off or, if you must wear one, choose one which is very different |

from usual (hand-painted nude for the old school tie or vice versa).

Put on a formal suit if you don't usually wear one. Try casual dress if you usually wear a suit. If you wear a suit, embellish the accessories such as shirts, handkerchiefs, cuff-links. Buy the latest style of suit in a different colour/pattern than usual.

As with all these experiments take careful note of:

—How you feel beforehand;

—How you feel during the introduction and implementation of the change;

—How other people react to you; and

—What you learn about yourself and the effects of change.

*Writing style*    Change it—somehow. Are you a brief or lengthy memo writer?

Are you conciliatory or aggressive in style? Are you serious or jokey?

Whatever you are or whatever your usual practice, try a change:

—Committee minutes which include some humour make more compelling reading.

Ask yourself the same questions as for 'dress'.

*Style of greeting*    This is a surprisingly powerful communicator. First, you must recognize your usual routine. Do you greet everyone from floor sweeper to MD effusively and at length or do you sneak to your office avoiding the eyes of everyone?

Select a new approach and try it out. Give your friends a brief and businesslike greeting and go and chat at length with caretakers and cleaners. Buttonhole the MD in the lift and pass the time of day with him.

Ask yourself the same before, during, and after questions.

For all these experiments give yourself a few minutes of peace and reflection to extract the most from the experience.

*Experiment 4: An unpleasant situation*

This is the most difficult of the experiments and it is therefore recommended to graduates of the earlier ones.

Choose a situation which you know from experience you will probably not enjoy and would normally avoid.

This might be as simple as digging the garden or cleaning the lounge, or it might be more complex, like spending the whole evening on your own in a bar, or deliberately spending some time with a colleague whom you dislike.

1. List some situations which you find unpleasant and try to avoid.

2. Pick one and deliberately put yourself into it.

3. Record your feelings on paper—before
                                                —during
                                                —afterwards

4. Write a short story changing the outcome of the experience.

5. Identify how much personal responsibility you feel for what happened or did not happen?

## FOLLOW-UP

If you enjoyed these experiments and learned something about risk taking and the effects of change, generate some ideas for yourself about things you'd like to change—about yourself, about other people.

Plan how you're going to go about these changes.

If you would like to read about change and its effects, *Future Shock* by Alvin Toffler (Pan, 1973) is a good easy read on the effects of change on all aspects of society. On the more specific management of change, an interesting book is *Managing with People: A Manager's Guide to Organisation Development* by Jack Fordyce and Raymond Weil (Addison-Wesley, 1971). You will also find useful *People at Work* by Dave Francis and Mike Woodcock (University Associates Press, 1975).

## REFERENCES
1.  Hampden-Turner, C., *Radical Man*, Duckworth, 1975.

# Activity 27
## Action planning

Action planning is an essential element in the process of learning or accomplishing. With small tasks or problems it is often an automatic process—'from my experience now, the next time I meet this, I'll do it that way'. There is often no need to verbalize or make conscious this process if it is working well.

With bigger problems or tasks automatic systems are rarely adequate. Sometimes, encouraged by their success with small, perhaps mechanical tasks, people will jump into action before they have planned sufficiently.* This may lead them to neglect big issues in the cause of solving many small ones. Another mistake is to think and plan rigorously, but never be quite ready to get down to action.

These problems occur when one is personally faced with a large task. In joint endeavours with other people, action planning is usually a formal requirement built into minutes or agreements—'George Evans will contact Philip Smith and report back to the next meeting on 15 March'. This is a form of contract between the people involved, the minutes or record being negotiated agreement to do specific things at specific times. Where an action plan doesn't exist in written form, joint endeavours only flourish where the action plan is recognized and members take personal responsibility for implementing it.

So here we have the essential elements of an action plan. It consists of setting targets or objectives to accomplish some action or actions; establishing standards of quality or time which act as deadlines *and taking or allocating personal responsibility for these actions.* How often do you say 'Oh, well, I meant to do it but I never got round to it'? In a competitive situation, your customer will go to someone who *does* get around to it. When you write an action plan you voluntarily commit yourself to a course of action which you will achieve to a certain standard or by a certain date. It

* But, see Activity 7 'Decision Making' for the case against detailed planning before action.

is this *commitment* which is the important aspect of an action plan. Planning is useless without commitment.

## Activity

The activity takes you through an action planning sequence with a worked example. You should choose your own example and work it through in parallel.

There are five stages:

1. Setting goals
2. Establishing sub-goals
3. Target dates
4. Resources/methods
5. Standards

You can use a shorter version, stages 1 to 3, if you prefer.

*Step 1*

Draw up a chart upon which to detail your action plan. It should have five vertical columns (three if you are using the short method) and look something like Table A27.1.

| Goals | Sub-goals | Target completion dates | Resources/ methods | Standards |
|-------|-----------|-------------------------|--------------------|-----------|
|       |           |                         |                    |           |

*Table A27.1.  Action plan chart*

*Step 2*

Choose a problem or task which you are working on or, preferably, about to start working on. Are you the sort of person who makes lists? Lists for shopping, for jobs to do this weekend; for telephone calls to make today. If so, you should have little difficulty in choosing a task. If you don't habitually make lists, try doing one now.

—Suppose you are told to clear your desk in preparation for a top priority job which is coming in a month's time:

—List all the things you would have to do in order to get your desk clear by then.

—Now choose the *most difficult* task on that list.

Write your tasks in the left-hand column of the Action Plan Chart. The example used here is an appraisal one:

TASK: Appraise the work section.

*Step 3*

Large tasks have a way of looking impossible, which is why most of us use every opportunity to avoid them. Setting sub-goals involves breaking up the main tasks into manageable proportions. They are often also the means by which the major goal is achieved, so in the case of our worked example:

*Major goal:* Appraising the work section

*Sub-goals:* (a) Memo reminding all concerned of annual appraisal.
   (b) Interviews with:
     Rose Smith;
     Jean Couldwell;
     George Evans;
     Bill Clark;
     David Salmon.
   (c) Complete documentation and circulate for agreement.
   (d) Make returns to personnel department.
   (e) Make individual action plans for any training needs arising out of appraisal.

Are you managing to work *your* chosen goal into sub-goals?
Questions which might throw up sub-goals are:

   —'What are the ways in which I could attain my goal?'

   —'What is involved in this task?'

Fill in these sub-goals in the second column of the Action Plan Chart.

*Step 4*

Setting target dates is straightforward. Set them for your sub-goals first and then estimate the likely date for your overall goal. You may have a deadline already, in which case you will have to plan sub-goal deadlines to help you reach this.

Fill in target completion dates on your Action Plan Chart. Remember these are your deadlines—failure to achieve them requires explanation—to yourself or to others.

If you're using the short Action Plan, you are now complete. Read the next two steps to see what isn't in your plan.

*Step 5*

The resources and methods column answers the questions:

'How am I going to tackle this problem?'

'What alternative courses of action are open to me?'

'What assistance do I need and what can I get?'

In our example, resources include:

(a) Appropriate documentation from personnel dept.

(b) Notes on appraisal interviewing from last management course.

(c) Any other useful things in personnel and Training, e.g., films, checklists, tips, etc.?

(d) Jack Williamson (source of advice).

Methods include:

(a) Circulating via internal post where appropriate and possible.

(b) Personal interviews (allow $1\frac{1}{2}$ hours for each).

Fill in resources and methods on your Action Plan Chart. In trying to complete this column you may discover you don't have sufficient resources and that you need to get these before proceeding. If so, obtaining these resources then becomes a sub-goal which precedes the others.

*Step 6*

When you have completed the Action Plan Chart, subject it to critical appraisal. Do this yourself or, perhaps better, get someone who knows about you and the task, to do it for you. Examples of the searching questions to ask are:

—'Is this goal really important for your department?'

—'Will these sub-goals lead to achievement of the main goal?'

By now you have an Action Plan Chart, see Table A27.2.

| 1. *Goals* | 2. *Sub-goals* | 3. *Target completion dates* | 4. *Resources/ methods* | 5. *Standards* |
|---|---|---|---|---|
| 1. Appraising the work section | | 31 January | | Sub-goal 2:<br>1. Develop personal, private, and confidential climate |
| | 1. Memo to all concerned | 4 Jan. | *Resources:*<br>1. Documentation (personnel) | 2. End each interview only after: |
| | 2. Interviews:<br>Rose Smith<br>Jean Couldwell<br>George Evans<br>Bill Clark<br>David Salmon | 18 Jan.<br>19 Jan.<br>20 Jan.<br>21 Jan.<br>22 Jan. | 2. Appraisal notes (last course)<br>3. Anything else in personnel, films, etc.? | (a) got all information<br>(b) I feel I've improved relationship<br>(c) each interviewee has said all; been satisfied or agreed a course of action. |
| | 3. Complete documentation and circulate | 22 Jan. | 4. Jack Williamson | |
| | 4. Make returns to personnel | 29 Jan. | *Methods:*<br>—Internal post<br>—Personal interviews ($1\frac{1}{2}$ hrs each) | Sub-goal 3:<br>Seek *commitment* rather than mere compliance |
| | 5. Make individual action plans on any identified training needs | say, by 1 March | | Sub-goal 4:<br>Ensure correctness to avoid return of documents<br><br>Sub-goal 5:<br>Action plans to conform to specification |

*Table A27.2. Completed action plan chart*

—'Can that time target be shortened?'

—'Will those performance standards tell you how well you're doing?

FOLLOW-UP

You can draw up an Action Plan Chart for any number of tasks or goals. It will give you a clear picture of what is involved in the completion of any complex task and also supply the discipline and commitment necessary for the completion of that task. This activity is similar to others in this book concerned with planning and analysis. If you have not done so already, try Activity 7 'Decision Making'; Activity 8 'Planning and Decision-Making Techniques' or any of several others related to this area.

If you want to explore the concept of action planning further, there are ideas to be gained from a study of the process of Management by Objectives. (MbO) which is a sophisticated system of managerial target setting and review which is not the same as action planning but which shares basic principles. Most general management books will have something to say about MbO, but specific references are: *The Practice of Management* by P. F. Drucker (Pan, 1969); in particular chapter 11 'Management by objectives and self-control; *Management by Objectives* by J. W. Humble (British Institute of Management, 1972). *Improving Business Results* by John Humble (McGraw-Hill, 1968). The British Institute of Management also has several other publications on MbO.

# Activity 28
## Accepting other people's ideas

LEARNING AREAS: CREATIVITY: Analytical skills: Self-knowledge

Most of us are all too familiar with occasions when we put forward new ideas—to the boss or to experts from other departments—only to find them blocked or rejected without fair hearing. Two of the activities in this book are designed to help you in such situations: Activity 11 'Planning Change' and Activity 9 'Choosing Solutions with a Chance'.

How often is the boot on the other foot? How often do you, as someone else's boss, or as an expert, reject ideas without a fair hearing? We suspect that this might happen more often than you imagine.

**The activity**

Look out for occasions on which you turn down other people's ideas. Often these people will be subordinate to you, but there may sometimes be other managers involved.

*Step 1*

On each occasion write down a list of as many possible reasons as you can think of as to why you reject an idea. Be open and honest. Write them down without qualification, evaluation, or discussion. Such a list might include:

—The idea is impractical.

—It is too expensive.

—It is administratively inconvenient.

—It challenges your basic beliefs.

—It renders irrelevant, redundant, or null-and-void the work in which you have already invested time and energy.

—It will cause you a lot of administrative or political headaches.

—It involves risks that you yourself are not prepared to take.

—You just don't like/respect the person putting forward the idea.

192

—It makes you feel unnecessary, redundant; it devalues your ideas or your role.

—You can't accept that other people in general, or this person in particular, can have better ideas than you.

—It causes you to lose face, to backtrack on previously stated ideas or beliefs.

—You don't want this other person to take credit.

*Step 2*

Look over the reasons you have given. Challenge them. Cross-examine yourself. Imagine you are a barrister challenging a witness (yourself). For example:

'How do you know it's impracticable? Have you tried it? What happened? Why? Why not?'

'What do you mean, too expensive? What are the detailed costs and benefits? How could it be done cheaper? It's your job to be able to do this, isn't it?'

'Are you sure you are not rejecting this idea because of the person who made it? What would you say if I pointed out that you nearly always reject ideas put forward by this person? Why is this?'

And so on.

This technique of self cross-examination can be very powerful. (It is a particular version of Activity 39 'Conversations with Yourself'.)

*Step 3*

What you do next is very much dependent on your 'verdict' following self-examination. Having identified some of the *real* reasons why you are blocking/rejecting the idea, you will need to explore these further—with yourself and with the other people concerned. Draw up a list of changes that you will make in response to an idea ('I will try, with the others concerned, to *make* the thing practicable, to *cut* its cost, to *overcome* administrative/political difficulties.')

FOLLOW-UP

The most important follow-up is to incorporate this way of responding into your normal everyday managerial behaviour. In this way you will increase the effectiveness of both yourself and your colleagues.

# Activity 29
## Brainstorming

One of the blocks that gets in the way of creative problem solving is that of making premature judgements. We often think of novel solutions or ideas, but, simply because they are unusual, we reject them immediately as nonsensical, impracticable, too expensive, and so on; the 'yes, but . . .' syndrome.

Another common block is that of narrow vision, or stereotyping. Because we are used to doing things in a certain way, we close our minds to alternatives, so that after a time they just never occur to us.

Brainstorming is a technique designed to overcome these two blocks to creative thinking. It can be done individually or in a group. We will describe first how to brainstorm on your own, and then make one or two points about doing it in a group.

### Activity

To get a good idea of the nature of brainstorming, we will use a fairly unimportant problem as an example.

### Step 1

Write down the answer to the following question:

'What are paper clips used for ?'

### Step 2

Unless you are a relatively fluent and innovative thinker, you will almost certainly have written only one or two uses for paper clips. You will almost certainly have said something about 'holding two or more pieces of paper together'.

194

Now write down, in five minutes, as many *other possible* uses of paper clips as you can think of. Don't worry how unusual, peculiar, or odd some of these might be. Write them down and keep thinking of more until the five minutes is up.

Clearly, there is no right answer, and individual lists will be very different. You will probably have come up with between 10 and 30 possible uses.

Look for the sort of attributes of paper clips that you have used. They have hooking/linking properties (e.g., chains; hooks; use for unlocking a car door through a partly open window); they can be straightened out (use as axles, spindles, spigots); they have sharp ends (for punching small holes, use as a defensive weapon—in an attacker's face or eye; as a cigar cutter, as a cocktail stick); they are flexible (use as binding wire); they conduct electricity (contact maker, fuse, various electrical connections); they are magnetic (use with a magnet, for picking up light ferrous objects from narrow or bent holes). The more attributes you have made use of in your list, then the greater the extent to which you have overcome the stereotyping problem.

The act of forcing the pace and making a quick list also helps to overcome the premature evaluation blockage. At this stage, there isn't time to think of reservations or 'yes, but's'.

Now think of a real problem facing you. Again, without pausing for evaluation, force yourself to list as many possible solutions as you can. Don't at this stage allow yourself to consider all the implications, pros and cons, of each solution. Just get a good list—the longer the better.

Now is the time for evaluating these possible solutions. Take each in turn, try to remain open-minded about them, consider all the strengths, weaknesses, consequences, requirements, and implications. You might find Activities 11 ('Planning Change'), 9 ('Choosing Solutions with a Chance'), and 27 ('Action Planning') particularly useful here.

Brainstorming can be used very effectively in groups. The problem is stated and each member shouts out possible solutions, which are written up on a blackboard or, preferably, flip chart by a member acting as scribe. During this process it is vital that no evaluation takes place. This prohibition applies to such subtle evaluations as laughing, expressions of wonder, amazement, approval, and derision. It is only when ideas are exhausted, and a very full list has been prepared, that careful, considered evaluation should be attempted.

If you are interested in reading more about creativity, three excellent books are *Creativity in Industry* by P. R. Whitfield (Penguin, 1975); *Conceptual Blockbusting* by J. L. Adams (W. H. Freeman, 1974); and *Synectics* by W. J. J. Gordon (Harper and Row, 1961). The latter describes in detail one particular approach to creative problem solving, while each of the other two gives a very good overview of creativity, illustrated with numerous examples and exercises.

# Activity 30
## Approaches to creativity

Many techniques and approaches have been suggested for creative solutions to problems. Some of these are simply ways of kicking yourself into seeing something new, or in regarding something familiar in a new way. Here are a few of them:

*Draw the problem:* Whether or not it is obviously a visual or spatial problem, try to represent it in pictorial/cartoon form, be as uninhibited as you can. Then consider possible solutions, or topics related to the problem, and draw them.

*Be the problem, or part of it:* For example, imagine that you are the troublesome part of a machine, or an object that has got lost or broken, or a message that was misunderstood. Think hard about what it would feel like, what could be done, what would help.

*Imagine something completely different:* Think of, imagine, anything—an object, an event, an idea. A spider's web, for instance, or a football match, or dissolving. Concentrate on this in relation to the problem at hand. You may spot a link, or get a fresh perspective that will help solve the problem.

*Invert the problem:* Turn the problem inside out or upside down, or reverse it. For example, instead of putting a product into a package, consider putting a package round a product; instead of protecting employees from an industrial accident, protect the accident from the staff.

*Turn the problem into an opportunity:* There is a corny saying 'every problem is an opportunity', but it is very often true.

*Write a story:* Fictionalize the problem and the people concerned with it. You could get a completely new angle on the situation.

Activity

Think of one or more real problems from your work situation. Try each of the approaches on it:

Draw it.
Be the problem.
Imagine something completely different.
Invert the problem.
Think of the opportunities that could arise from the problem.
Write the story.
Then note down possible solutions and useful ideas.

In the light of the ideas you generate, reflect on which of the approaches helped you the most. Think of, and try out, other approaches. You will find it useful, and truly interesting, to carry out what may seem at first a rather silly exercise, but we guarantee that you will come up with new ideas and imaginative/creative solutions.

## FOLLOW-UP

Try some of this book's other activities for developing creativity. Above all, to become truly creative you must let yourself go a little. For some useful books, see the list following Activity 29 'Brainstorming'. Look at, too, *Lateral Thinking for Management* by Edward de Bono (McGraw-Hill, 1971). An interesting book which deals with a technique for drawing problems is *Illuminative Incident Analysis* by Cortazzi and Roote (McGraw-Hill, 1975).

# Activity 31
## Attribute alternatives

We are often unable to think of new ways of doing things simply because we are locked in by constraints imposed by our assumptions about the way things should be done. One way of trying to overcome these constraints is to identify the attributes of the current method, and then generate a list of alternative attributes.

*Activity*

*Step 1*

Note down the method or device currently in use, with its main characteristics and attributes.

For example—from the dairy industry. Shortage of milk bottles is forcing us to consider alternative containers.

Current container: bottle.

Attributes: glass; returnable; bottle shape; capacity one pint.

*Step 2*

Take each of the attributes and consider alternatives to it. At this stage, use the 'Brainstorming' rules (Activity 29). List any alternatives that come to mind and do not attempt to evaluate them. No matter how silly or impractical it seems, list it.

Keeping with our example, we might generate the following alternatives:

Made of: (glass) paper; plastic; wood; aluminium; steel; cardboard; pottery.

Life: (returnable) Disposable.

Shape: (bottle) bag; cube; triangle; sphere; hexagon; cylinder; pipe.

Capacity: (1 pint) litre; $\frac{1}{2}$ pint; 100 cc; 10 cc.

*Step 3*

Examine and evaluate the alternatives. We can consider any combinations, often involving hundreds of permutations. In practice we usually look at some of the more likely combinations.

These must be examined for practicability. Ideas might be logically or technically feasible but have to be ruled out on grounds of cost, say, or market acceptability. Triangular, waxed paper milk cartons, for instance, have still not really caught on in the UK: housewives don't like them. Some dairies experimented with milk delivered in one-pint plastic bags—each household being provided with a special jug into which the bag is placed for pouring.

## FOLLOW-UP

Keep trying out this exercise with real problems. Remember the important rule: generate as many alternatives as possible but leave evaluation until later. If you would like to read more about this subject, three excellent books on creativity are: *Creativity in Industry* by P. R. Whitfield (Penguin, 1975); *Conceptual Blockbusting* by J. L. Adams (W. H. Freeman, 1974); and *Synectics* by W. J. J. Gordon (Harper and Row, 1961).

# Activity 32
## Coping with complexity

LEARNING AREAS: MENTAL AGILITY: Emotional resilience

We have mentioned Alvin Toffler[1] before in this book. He suggested that the stress and disorientation that can be induced by subjecting people to too much change in too short a time is a sickness from which many of us are already suffering. He is concerned that we know so little about adapting to change, and his book was an attempt to start us thinking.

Coping and adapting to change requires effort in terms of new skills, new knowledge, and emotional stability. We do not here attempt to deal with all of these, but concentrate on that aspect which we call 'mental agility' or 'flexible intelligence'. The concept of intelligence is complex and worrying for most people, who connect it with crude tests which we used to give 11-year-old children.

The intelligence or agility we talk about here is an ability, potential or realized, which everyone has to some extent. It can be improved with practice like any other skill. It is the ability which allows us to do several things at once, switching our minds and resources from one topic to another, making hundreds of decisions as we do so, storing information, recalling it—in short what all of us do when working in a multi-task situation.

Does a mother's job require the exercise of flexible intelligence? If you doubt it—try this:

Cook a breakfast for four people *at the same time as*:

> finding and putting together two lots of dinner money;
> cleaning two pairs of shoes;
> listening to the news on the radio;
> brushing two lots of hair;
> talking lovingly to spouse;
> talking lovingly to children;
> dealing with sundry contingencies
> —all in 30 minutes.

How did you get on?

Your work is probably just as complex but you do it instinctively, and therefore without learning how to apply a general skill to new situations. A teacher in a classroom, a foreman in a machine shop, a manager at a meeting all pursue a number of tasks, observing thousands of stimuli and attending to a few, making many responses and so on—often without much conscious thought about the complexity of the situation.

To help you learn how to respond to new complexity and the contingencies which seem to form an increasing part of every manager's job, try this.

### Activity

There are two versions. You are asked to work on certain tasks, thinking consciously about how you are adapting to the skill requirements involved in doing several tasks at once.

### Step 1

Make provision for spending a free hour on this activity. Choose six suitable tasks. If you are doing the exercise in the office, tasks might be:

  —doing *The Times* crossword;

  —writing a paper or notes ready for a meeting;

  —planning your work objectives for the next six months;

  —telephoning three or four people you need to contact;

  —talking to a colleague/your secretary about something which interests him/her;

  —preparing statistics/filling government forms (an Inland Revenue form would be ideal!);

  —planning the best, new arrangement of furniture in your office;

  —reading a behavioural science book on management.

Whenever you are at home, on a train journey, in a hotel, choose tasks that are related to that particular circumstance.

### Step 2

(a) Estimate how long each task will take; add up the total time and halve it. (You only ever have half the time you need.)

Now, try to complete all the tasks in that time. Don't do them sequentially, try to do them together, switching from one to the other.

(b) If you find it hard to switch from one task to another, number them 1 to 6; divide your allotted time by a multiple of 6 (12 or 18 say) and, using a dice, change tasks after every one-twelfth or one-eighteenth of your time. For example, if you had allocated 60 minutes, dividing this by 18 will give you approximately 3. Every 3 minutes roll the dice and take up the indicated task. You can switch up to 18 times in a hour, on 6 tasks.

*Step 3*

Give yourself time to think about the following questions. Take each question in turn and note down your responses.

(a) *What did I actually achieve in terms of completing the tasks?*

(b) *What feelings did I have while doing the tasks?* (Simply jot down as many phrases/adjectives that spring to mind.)

(c) *Have I ever felt like this before?*

*If so, when and where was it? What was the outcome?*

(d) *Could I have been better organized or better prepared? (If so, how would you go about it next time?)*

(e) *Could I increase my ability to deal with multi-task situations?*

If your answer to (e) is 'yes', repeat this experiment in many situations. Remember that the most important thing is to be consciously aware of what you are doing and when you are doing it, and to give yourself time for reflection afterwards. Without this you will miss the learning potential inherent in your own experience of a situation.

## FOLLOW-UP

If you are interested in this type of intelligence exercise, try *A 5-Day Course in Thinking* by Edward de Bono (Penguin Books, 1969). Most psychology texts have a chapter devoted to a general description of the concept of intelligence and its development. A good example is *Social Psychology* by Roger Brown, chapter 5, 'The development of intelligence', pages 197–245 in the 1968 edition (Collier-Macmillan).

## REFERENCES

1. Toffler, A., *Future Shock*, Pan, 1973.

# Activity 33
## Quick thinking

LEARNING AREAS: MENTAL AGILITY: Social skills

In all the research on effective management, the only characteristic found to consistently predict success is some measure of general intelligence.

The nature of managerial work demands the ability to think through complex matters, to think quickly on one's feet, and to switch rapidly from one problem to another.

There is a widely held popular belief that intelligence is an innate human characteristic which cannot be developed through training. This idea is taken from early psychological theories which have long since been questioned and rejected. Current thinking on the question is complicated, but it is clear that the kind of mental abilities that make up intelligence can improve significantly through experience and practice. The following activity is designed to give you practice in thinking quickly on your feet.

*Activity*

You need ten filing cards or small pieces of paper, and a tape recorder.

*Step 1*

Write one of the following topics on each of five cards:

    Pay policy
    Productivity
    Consumerism
    Industrial relations
    Safety

*Step 2*

Write one of the following types of audience on each of the remaining five cards:

    Group of trade union officials
    Party of visiting Japanese business men

The sixth form of your local school
Party of American tourists
Group of old age pensioners/senior citizens

Shuffle each of the sets of cards separately and put them face downwards so that you do not know what order they are in.

*Step 3*

Turn on the tape recorder. Pick up the first card on each pile and talk for one minute on the topic revealed, to the audience as turned up from the cards. After a minute, pick up the second topic and audience cards and talk for another minute. Repeat this until you have used all the cards.

Play back the tape to review how well you did in keeping to the topic and relating it to the audience in each instance.

Re-shuffle the cards and repeat the activity. Think up additional topics and types of audience if these become over-familiar.

FOLLOW-UP

Thinking skills come with practice, so the more you can exercise them, the more they will develop.

You should be able to find plenty of opportunities for this in the context of your work. If you want further exercises to work at, and would like to know how your intelligence compares with the population in general, try: *Check Your Own I.Q.* by H. J. Eysenck (Penguin, 1966).

# Activity 34
## Developing a helicopter mind

LEARNING AREAS: MENTAL AGILITY: Balanced learning habits: Creativity

An extensive study of managers in one large organization concluded that a quality called 'a helicopter mind' is a key determinant of successful management. 'Helicopter mind' means an ability to think in both concrete and abstract terms, and to move rapidly between the two, linking abstract ideas to specific ideas for action. Managers who think in this way are good at linking theory to practice so that each improves the other.

What determines whether thinking moves 'up' to the abstract, or 'down' to the specific, is the kind of question with which one is faced. In general, 'why?' questions move up, and 'how?' questions move down. You can ask 'how?' and 'why?' about *activities* and *statements of 'fact'*. For example, selecting people for jobs can be analysed this way:

WHY?—To produce enough to meet orders.
↑
WHY?—To get good enough people to work the machines.
↑
TASK—SELECT PEOPLE FOR JOBS.
↓
HOW?—Assess skills needed, test applicants for these.
↓
HOW?—Study existing staff, develop tests to demonstrate skills.

Having answered 'why?' questions it is possible to move down again with 'how?' questions, and develop alternative solutions:

TASK—To produce enough to meet orders.
↓
HOW?—Get more people to work machines OR get faster machines.
↓
HOW?—Offer overtime OR recruit more people.

If one starts with a 'statement of fact', one can ask:

WHY is this true?

and

HOW can this be applied?

For example:

Figure A34.1

Again, asking 'how?' questions after 'why?' questions can generate new alternatives and ideas.

## Activity

Practise analysing *activities* and *facts* relevant to your work activities, using both 'how?' and 'why?' questions.

A good way to do this is to write down the activity or fact in the middle of a large blank piece of paper and build answers to 'how?' and 'why?' questions around it. It will look something like Fig. A34.2.

In doing the activity, and in your thinking in general, you should aim to think in terms of 'how?' and 'why?' rather than mainly in terms of one or the other.

## FOLLOW-UP

You may find it useful to use some of your how/why analyses as the basis for discussion with others who share the same concerns.

Broad reading of things which you may regard as 'academic', 'theoretical', or 'philosophical' may add to your stock of abstract ideas that you can relate to the specifics of your work activities. Libraries and educational institutions are good sources of these.

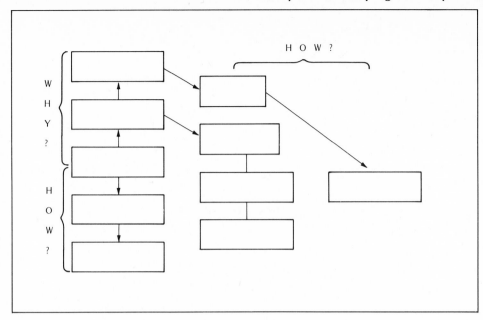

*Figure A34.2*

If you are interested in pursuing the matter of linking theory to practice, you will find *Zen and the Art of Motorcycle Maintenance* by Robert Pirsig (Corgi, 1976) a mind-stretching book to read.

# Activity 35
## Managing your dependency

LEARNING AREAS: BALANCED LEARNING HABITS

The theme of this book is *self-development* and that for real learning to occur you must take personal responsibility for your own learning.

In a sense we are urging you to move from:

*Dependence*—accepting uncritically what teachers and people with formal authority over you may present as the 'right way' to do things.

to:

*Independence*—taking instructions from teachers and authority figures as suggestions which you may try out and evaluate for yourself, adding them to your repertoire of skills and practices if *you* judge them to work.

However, the *independence* philosophy can easily be overdone and lead to a kind of obstinate unwillingness to accept help and guidance from people well qualified to give it. The properly independent person may make extensive use of *mature dependency*—making full use of advice and help from others with genuine expertise and experience. For wisdom to be passed from person to person and generation to generation, so that the benefit of others' past successes and failures can be passed on, mature dependency must play a part.

Activity
*Step 1*

Make a list of six or so major tasks or activities which you have to perform in your work: preparing budgets, negotiating and bargaining, designing new products or procedures, providing leadership for a team or group, advising others, selling things or ideas, planning operations, interviewing and so on. Write them down in the first column of Table A35.1.

*Step 2*

Taking each of these tasks or activities in turn, go through each of the following questions, stopping when you feel you can answer 'yes' to one of them. Record your answer by putting a tick under the first question to

| Task/ activity | Are you an expert? | Do you know of an expert? | Do you believe an expert exists? | Or is it an, as yet, unsolved problem? |
|---|---|---|---|---|
|  |  |  |  |  |
|  |  |  |  |  |
|  |  |  |  |  |
|  |  |  |  |  |
|  |  |  |  |  |
|  |  |  |  |  |

*Table A35.1*

which you can answer 'yes' for each task or activity. There should be only one tick for each task or activity.

(a) In terms of practical ability to carry out this task or activity, do you believe that you are expert at it, in the sense that there is no one else who can do it better than you and that you can reliably deal with it?

(b) If not, is there an expert or source of expertise, that you know of who/ which does or could provide you with help on this task?

(c) If not, do you believe that somewhere there is a procedure, technique, approach, or person which/who can provide a reliable solution to carrying out the task?

(d) If not, presumably you must regard this as one of those tasks or problems for which, at the moment, no known solution exists, and you have as good a chance as anyone else of finding one?

*Step 3*

Now treat each of your answers as a statement to be *tested*. Consider what *evidence* you have. Are you really fully competent? Can the 'expert' really produce results? Can you track down an expert or authoritative source of knowledge on the problem?

It will be particularly useful if you show your conclusions to someone else who is familiar with the same tasks and problems, and who will give you an honest opinion about your conclusions.

## FOLLOW-UP

You may find it useful to follow up this exercise with some exploration into what expertise there is around to deal with problems you are facing. There may be sources within your own organization, in libraries, or in educational institutions in your area, for instance.

Consider whether your personality leads you to believe in, seek out, and rely on experts, or whether you tend to go it alone; and whether this helps or hinders you.

Consider, and discuss with colleagues, whether your organization has a culture of relying on experts or in finding its own solutions, and whether this is functional or not.

# Activity 36
## Understanding your learning processes

LEARNING AREAS: BALANCED LEARNING HABITS: Self-knowledge: Sensitivity to
events

There are five stages to learning a new skill or ability:

—Feeling a need for new behaviour and becoming aware of
inadequacies in the way you do things.

—Identifying the behaviours involved in a new skill or activity.

—Practising these behaviours.

—Seeking and getting feedback on your performance.

—Integrating the behaviours into your repertoire of skills and abilities.

This activity aims to get you thinking about how you acquired your existing
repertoire of skills and abilities. Being able to learn from everyday
experience is a skill in itself, and the need for this ability grows daily. Until
recently, the most popular theories about learning were those which
suggested that much of our adult behaviour was learned in the first five years
of life. More recently, we have become aware of the need and potential for
continuing education, beyond the formal years of schooling. Lifelong
education is especially vital for managers whose responsibilities demand that
they cope with and manage accelerating change.

Learning to learn is therefore an activity on which it is worth spending time.
It will help you ultimately with everything you need or want to learn in the
future.

In this activity, you are asked to look at some examples of where you have
been successful as a manager; what skills or abilities helped you to be
successful; and how you acquired those skills.

## Activity

*Step 1*

Think of two incidents in the past year where you have been successful as a manager. These are 'high spots' or 'peak experiences'—the sort of thing you would talk about in a promotion interview to demonstrate your strengths. Now describe these events—what actually happened and what did you do exactly? Write these down and be as *specific* as you can.

## INCIDENT 1

What happened?

What did you do?

## INCIDENT 2

What happened?

What did you do?

Looking at what you did in these two cases, what were the key *skills* and *qualities* within yourself that enabled you to do what you did and to achieve a successful outcome? Write these down in column 1 of Table A36.1. Then answer these two questions:

(a)  *Where* did I learn it from?

    —from the boss?
    —from school?
    —from doing the job?
    —from a book?
    —from my colleagues? etc.

You will also find it useful to recall over what period of time and at what stage in your life this skill/ability was learned. You can do this by remembering the latest time when you are sure you *did not* have the skill/ability and the earliest time you *did*.

(b)  *How* did I learn it? i.e., what process was involved?

    —by being told something?
    —by imitating somebody?
    —by puzzling it out for myself?
    —by accident or on purpose?
    —through emotional or intellectual channels? etc.

Take a blank sheet of paper and write down all the insights you have had so far about *how* you learn. Use the data generated in Steps 1 and 2.

When you have got down as much as you can, consider the following

| Skill/ability | Where did I learn it from? | How did I learn it? |
|---|---|---|
| 1. | | |
| 2. | | |
| 3. | | |
| 4. | | |
| 5. | | |
| 6. | | |

Table A36.1

questions about your learning processes. Write down any additional insights you get as a result of answering these questions.

(a) How well do the five stages of learning a new skill or ability fit with your experience of your learning?

(b) Do you learn different things in different ways; if so, what things and what ways?

(c) Think about other people you know well and how they learn. Are there any processes which you do not use?

(d) Does receiving 'inputs'—being told or shown something, figure in your learning processes?

(e) Does imitating other people, or learning by observing the success and failures of their actions, figure in your learning processes?

(f) What is the place of emotion and feelings in your learning? Is learning painful, pleasant, or what?

*Step 4*

This will test your understanding of how you learn and also make some demands on your creativity and ingenuity. *You need a clear 30 minutes for this step:*

(a) Choose a personal skill or ability which you would like to improve.

(b) Spend *10 minutes* designing a very small learning event for yourself. It should last not more than 10 minutes. Use any resources you see around you and all the insights gained from analysing your past learning experiences. Be prepared to be adventurous, creative, and open to the experience which will happen.

(c) Do the learning exercise. Keep to the 10 minutes.

(d) Evaluate the experience for 10 minutes:

> —Did it work?
> —Why did it work (or not work)?
> —What increased understandings do you have about your learning processes?

FOLLOW-UP

Learning how to learn is not easy but it is, perhaps, the ultimate management skill. Understanding your learning processes is one way to improve your ability to learn. Work on this, and the rest of the managerial skills and abilities come much more easily.

If you prefer to reflect and think a little before trying more activities in the light of what you have learned about your own learning processes, do so; you are the director of your own learning programme.

If you would like to read more about the way adults learn, the following books will be useful and interesting: *Adults Learning* by Jennifer Rogers (Penguin, 1971)—especially chapters 1, 2, and 3; *Adults in Education* edited by Jennifer Rogers (BBC Publications)—especially chapter 2 'Learning' by David James; *How Children Learn* by John Holt (Penguin, 1967)—very readable, gives many insights into adult learning.

# Activity 37
## Study skills

LEARNING AREAS: BALANCED LEARNING HABITS: Professional knowledge: Self-knowledge

We often say 'he is very bright' or 'she is very clever' about someone who is obviously well educated or highly qualified, implying that they are more able than the rest of us. Unfortunately, professional qualifications are often taken as a measure of a person's worth, and people of ability are handicapped by the lack of them. Intelligence or basic ability is only part of the game of obtaining professional qualifications; opportunity and chance often form as large a part. Another aspect is application—a most important aspect of which is skill at studying. Study skills are different from the other components of academic success because you are not born with them and you do not acquire them by chance. You have to learn them.

Study skills are important whether you are professionally qualified or not. They are important to all managers and they contribute to that illusive skill of being able to learn from one's own experience. Qualified managers may well have picked up study skills in the process of becoming qualified. Those who are unqualified or underqualified may find they are lacking a skill which can be remedied with time and effort.

Before going further, it is necessary to do some diagnosing to discover your own skills and deficiencies in this area.

Activity

We do not have the space here to make you proficient in all study skills, but it is possible to do some diagnosis and point you in the right direction. Complete Questionnaire 1 to get an estimate of your overall study skill level.

To evaluate yourself simply add up the circled numbers. The *very best* way to use this questionnaire is to complete it *prior* to some period of study, and then after to see if you feel you have made an improvement.

The measurement which matters is one which matches you against yourself and not against some mythical standard.

218

| | This is a big problem for me | This is something of a problem for me | This is not a problem for me |
|---|---|---|---|

For each question, circle one number—1, 2, or 3—in the columns at the right

Here are some tasks which have to be achieved for successful study.

'How difficult is it for you to . . .

| | This is a big problem for me | This is something of a problem for me | This is not a problem for me |
|---|---|---|---|
| 1. . . . decide on a suitable *place* for studying? | 3 | 2 | 1 |
| 2. . . . decide *when* to study, or for *how long*? | 3 | 2 | 1 |
| 3. . . . choose your goal, i.e., precisely what you want to learn? | 3 | 2 | 1 |
| 4. . . . decide *how* to achieve your goal, i.e., what study activities to perform? | 3 | 2 | 1 |
| 5. . . . obtain or reach people, books, and other *resources*? | 3 | 2 | 1 |
| 6. . . . deal with *lack of desire* for achieving your goal, once set? | 3 | 2 | 1 |
| 7. . . . deal with *dislike of activities* necessary to reach your goal, e.g., you want to learn Spanish but you hate reading? | 3 | 2 | 1 |
| 8. . . . cope with *doubts* about success | 3 | 2 | 1 |
| 9. . . . *estimate level of knowledge or skill*—start and finish and also during study to determine progress? | 3 | 2 | 1 |
| 10. . . . deal with *difficulty in understanding* some part or through lack of fundamental knowledge at some stage? | 3 | 2 | 1 |
| 11. . . . be able to *concentrate*? | 3 | 2 | 1 |
| 12. . . . be able to *remember*? | 3 | 2 | 1 |
| 13. . . . be able to *apply* knowledge gained to real life situations? | 3 | 2 | 1 |
| 14. . . . deal with *frustration* arising from speed of learning; material containing opinions rather than clear-cut 'facts'? | 3 | 2 | 1 |
| 15. . . . be able to overcome laziness or inertia despite interest? | 3 | 2 | 1 |
| 16. . . . find fellow learners for mutual stimulation and companionship?' | 3 | 2 | 1 |

*Table A37.1.  Questionnaire 1: study tasks*

However . . .

—if you scored less than *20* you have few study problems (at least as revealed by this questionnaire).

—if you scored between *20 and 30* you do have quite a few difficulties. Spending time on them will benefit you.

—if you scored over *30*, your innate ability is probably being held back through an inability to study.

BUT don't take too much notice of these notional numbers—this questionnaire is only as valid as *you* think it is. Go back through the questionnaire and look at the questions where you circled 3.

Then study the ones where you circled 2.

What does this add up to in terms of difficulty?

Answers will vary widely with individuals—you must puzzle out what yours mean. For example, an inability to concentrate or to maintain motivation (both very common study problems), may be caused by a huge variety of things. There may be a very simple reason such as working in a noisy or unsuitable environment; or it may be exceedingly complex. Lack of concentration is a frequent result of emotional upset, and lack of motivation may stem from a deep-seated fear of failure, perhaps developed in childhood.

We are not suggesting psychoanalysis as a means of interpreting your questionnaire answers—merely pointing out the wide variety of interpretations possible. You will certainly find it helpful to talk to someone whom you find supportive—preferably someone who has had some counselling experience—perhaps in the Personnel Department?

The sorts of solutions you might come to are:

—Set yourself a STUDY DIARY, giving specific periods on given days of the week for study.    (Questions 2; 6; 7; 11?; 15?

—Find your sort of place to study (this may be combined with time) e.g.,    (Questions 1; 2; 5; 15?; 16;)

—Establish a self-testing procedure.    (Questions 6; 8; 9;)

—Establish a rigorous PRACTICE ROUTINE    (Questions 11; 12; 7?; 6?)

—Join a suitable evening class.    (Questions 4; 5; 9; 10; 15?; 16)

—Consult an expert or tutor.    (Questions 4; 5; 9; 10;)

—Set yourself a detailed ACTION PLAN.    (Questions 3; 4; 5; 9;)

—Get a supportive or sympathetic ally to talk to from time to time—to bounce ideas off; to counsel; to encourage; to discipline, etc.    (All questions)

Remember, these are only a few of the possible solutions.

So far we have been talking about overall study tasks—the problems that have to be overcome when studying—usually alone and without a tutor. It is now time to move on to the specific skills involved in studying—reading, writing, and so on. Answer Questionnaire 2 (Table A37.2).

For each question circle on number—1, 2, or 3 in the columns at the right.

Here are some skills involved in successful study.

'Do you . . .

| | Rarely | Sometimes | Usually |
|---|---|---|---|
| 1. . . . decide in advance *what* you are going to study and *where*? | 1 | 2 | 3 |
| 2. . . . set yourself goals and sub-goals? e.g., I will read this book between now and then; 30 pages here, etc. | 1 | 2 | 3 |
| 3. . . . meet your deadlines—especially with regard to written work, reports, etc.? | 1 | 2 | 3 |
| 4. . . . read fast enough to read all the books you need to read on any given matter? | | | |
| 5. . . . skim or scan through books using contents pages and indexes, before deciding what to read? | 1 | 2 | 3 |
| 6. . . . consciously read for a purpose, i.e., to gain specific material and not just to "get everything"? | 1 | 2 | 3 |
| 7. . . . find it possible to concentrate when listening to lectures or talks? | 1 | 2 | 3 |
| 8. . . . take notes when listening to talks or lectures? | 1 | 2 | 3 |
| 9. . . . know how to use library systems to find the books or information you need? | 1 | 2 | 3 |
| 10. . . . write key notes i.e., headings and sub-headings rather than continuous prose? | 1 | 2 | 3 |
| 11. . . . feel at ease drawing up reports or writing papers? | 1 | 2 | 3 |
| 12. . . . express yourself well in writing?' | 1 | 2 | 3 |

*Table A37.2. Questionnaire 2: study skills*

This second questionnaire focuses on several key areas of study skill:

- —organizing yourself and your time;
- —reading;
- —listening to talks and lectures;
- —note-taking;
- —writing.

Obviously you will be helped a great deal in learning what you want to learn if you develop skills in these areas. In the questionnaire you should aim to be consistently circling 3's—if you have several 1's then these are weak areas for you. This is particularly so if you have two or three 1's in any one area, for example, questions 1, 2, and 3 all concern organization.

Study skills take time and purposeful practice to master. If this exercise has helped you to pinpoint or identify particular problems, you can begin to work on these by following up some of the following suggestions.

## FOLLOW-UP

On the specific study skills such as reading, note-taking, writing, and so on, *Learn how to Study* by Derek Rowntree (McDonald, 1970) is an excellent and extremely cheap 'best buy'. Written in programmed text form it has seven chapters: 'Why Learn to Study'; How to organize your studying'; 'How to tackle a text book'; 'How to write essays'; 'How to read better and faster'; 'How to make notes'; and 'How to deal with examinations'.

This really is a very good investment—attractive and easy to read. It also contains an excellent bibliography of other 'learn to study' books. In particular some rapid reading books are listed.

Another book which is provocative and stimulating around study is *Use Your Head* by Tony Buzan (BBC Publications, 1974). This is wider and less basic than Rowntree.

# Activity 38
## How do you learn?

LEARNING AREAS: BALANCED LEARNING HABITS: Self-knowledge: Sensitivity to events

You may have already completed Activities 36 'Understanding Your Learning Processes' and 37 'Study Skills' which helped you assess how proficient you are at the study skills. This activity is closely related to both the others but concentrates on the key experiences by which you have learned and do learn those things you need to learn. It increases your ability to learn how to learn, which is a major goal of this book.

In adults, learning takes place usually as a result of existing behaviour being seen by the learner as inadequate in the light of various experiences or things that happen to him or her. If the learner is open and willing to learn, examination of these experiences will provide clues as to how existing behaviour can be modified. Adults very rarely learn completely new behaviour—we have so much accumulated experience, some part of which will usually have a bearing on the problem at hand. Often this past experience gets in the way of learning new things: 'I have 10 years experience of interviewing, why should I go on a course?' Unexamined happenings in life are not experiences—merely things which happened and passed by without impact. Experience is something we reflect upon and which causes us to modify, often in small ways, our perception of situations and the way we behave in them.

This process[1]—which we call the significant learning process—looks something like Fig. A38.1.

Activity

Each of us is a unique blend of inherited characteristics modified over time by all sorts of experiences—some pleasant, many unpleasant. It is often the painful experiences that teach us so much.

To do this activity you need to re-live some of those past experiences. We're going to analyse them to find out just what features made them so important for you.

223

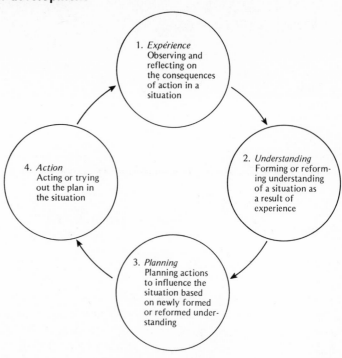

*Figure A38.1*

## Step 1

Think of the key learning experiences in your life—the experiences which you feel led to significant changes in your behaviour. They can be short or long experiences, but they must be followed by a discernible change in the way you behaved. Jot down now a title or phrase to label all the experiences which come to mind.

Here's a sample list:

—being sent away to school for the first time (1949);

—first love affair (1956);

—broken leg (1960);

—university degree (1971–74).

## Step 2

Take a piece of paper and draw horizontal lines across to divide it into eight equal parts. Use one sheet for each experience and label each sheet. In the eight parts answer the following questions:

1. *What happened?*

2. *What started it?*

3. *What did you learn?*

4. *What words describe how you felt while it was happening?*

5. *Who else was involved?*

6. *Did they help or hinder your learning? How?*

7. *How would you describe the learning process?*

8. *What were the key characteristics of this event—as compared with others in your life when you didn't learn as much?*

*Step 3*

(a) Look back through your learning experience sheets and seek out commonalities—commonalities in all senses—in how things started; in how you felt; in who was involved, etc.

Write these down.

Can you discern any patterns in your key learning experiences?

(b) Look back through your learning experience sheets and make two lists—one of factors which helped you to learn and one of factors which hindered your learning:

| Factors assisting learning | Factors hindering learning |
|---|---|
| (i). | (i) |
| (ii) | (ii) |
| (iii) | (iii) |
| (iv) | (iv) |
| (v) | (v) |
| (vi) | (vi) |

You should now have an enhanced view of the key learning experiences which have equipped you with the skills and abilities which you possess today. In particular you should know more about patterns in your key learning experiences and what helped and hindered your learning. If you managed to re-live some really painful experiences then you probably drew a good deal of insight out of them. Above all the activity should help you with *introspection*—a much underrated learning skill which allows you to extract the lessons from your own experience.

## FOLLOW-UP

If you got a lot out of this activity you may wish to continue straight on to Activity 36 'Understanding your Learning Processes' or Activity 37 'Study Skills' both of which are closely linked to this one.

## REFERENCE

1. Adapted from D. A. Kolb, I. M. Rubin, and J. M. McIntyre, *Organisational Psychology: An Experiential Approach*, 2nd Edition, Prentice Hall, 1974, p. 28.

# Activity 39
## Conversations with yourself

LEARNING AREAS: SELF-KNOWLEDGE: Creativity

Talking to yourself—according to schoolboy joke—is a sign of madness. Art historians will tell you that madness and creativity are closely linked and that what was sometimes described as lunacy we would now call non-conformity or even genius.[1] Each of us has observed abnormality in famous people—it is often this deviation from the norm which makes them creative and famous. There are clear links here with Liam Hudson's concept of 'divergent' as opposed to 'convergent' thinking[2] and de Bono's vertical and lateral thinking.[3]

Hopefully this book will not drive you mad, but a certain amount of experimentation and playfulness is necessary for creativity.

The following activity is very simple and straightforward. It is also very powerful. You'll need a tape recorder, a private room, and at least 30 minutes of uninterrupted time.

*Step 1*

Go into the room, lock the door, switch on the tape recorder and begin speaking to *yourself*. Do not address any audience or person, real or imaginary. Speak to yourself.

You will find this quite difficult and you may need several starts before you get into it. If you have any doubts, play back what you've said and check whether you are *really speaking to yourself.*

*Step 2*

When you have mastered talking to yourself you can start on any specific problem or difficult situation facing you. Keep talking until you have said everything you wish to say about this problem.

*Step 3*

Play back the tape. Listen until you are satisfied that you understand yourself.

*Step 4*

Wipe off the tape before leaving the room—whether you achieved Steps 2 and 3 in their entirety or not. *This is extremely important.*

*Step 5*

Repeat Steps 1 to 4 periodically as a means of getting in touch with the problem.

The theory is that whenever we speak, we speak to an audience. We always try to impress or achieve a specific effect upon another or others. We rarely, if ever, speak to ourselves to find out *what we really think.*

Creativity seems to be only partly a conscious process. There is only so much that can be done by conscious effort. Often that 'aha!' or 'eureka!' experience comes after we have slept on or dropped a problem to think about something else. The assumption is that our unconscious mind worked somehow on the original problem and emerged with a solution or break-through.

This activity is a formal way of 'thinking aloud'—a more respectable occupation than talking to yourself!

Try it—it may break that block you've been struggling with for so long.

## FOLLOW-UP

If you're interested in the problem of creativity and how to encourage it you may care to get hold of *Conceptual Blockbusting* by James Adams (Prentice Hall, 1975). This is a very readable and entertaining book from an engineer turned teacher and behavioural scientist. Another recent work on creativity and innovation in British industry is *Creativity in Industry* by P. R. Whitfield (Penguin, 1975).

## REFERENCES

1. Berger, J., *Ways of Seeing*, Penguin, 1972.
2. Hudson, L., *Contrary Imaginations*, Penguin, 1967.
3. de Bono, E., *The Use of Lateral Thinking*, Penguin, 1971.

# Appendix 1
## A note for management trainers

Although primarily intended for managers to use themselves, as a help in their own self-development, we hope that this book will also be used by management trainers and educators. The purpose of this short appendix is to suggest a few ways in which this might be done, together with some relevant references for further reading.

One way for trainers to use the activities is by incorporating them into existing programmes or courses. Either as an option or as an extra 'syllabus area', sessions can be devoted to working with some of the activities from the book. Alternatively, special short courses can be run, with self-development as the theme and the book providing some, or all, of the course resources.

The goals of self-development are highly individualized. We therefore strongly recommend that any course, or section of a course, that focuses on self-development should take an individualized, autonomous approach, such as a 'learning community'. The latter involves both participants and tutors in a number of phases:

—establishing a supportive learning climate;

—diagnosis and setting individual goals;

—generating, identifying, and sharing resources to meet these individual needs;

—making plans to meet as many of the various individual needs as possible;

—meeting the needs;

—continuous steering evaluation, right from the start, to ensure that the whole event is on course for meeting its goals.

These phases, with examples, are discussed in more detail in a number of papers, including Knowles,[1] Boydell,[2] Megginson and Pedler,[3] and Heron.[4] With the specific context of use with this book, they may be briefly elaborated thus:

## Establishing a supportive learning climate

Self-development is bound to be a risky business, involving as it does facing up to one's own weaknesses and trying to work on them. It is therefore extremely important to provide a learning climate that helps people to examine their own weaknesses, to discuss them, to practice new behaviours, to take risks, to give and receive feedback, and generally become deeply involved in the exciting, if sometimes painful, process of growth. This requires a high level of trust, mutual understanding and respect, and commitment both to one's own learning, and to that of others. Such climates are not characteristic of most groups when they first form, and one of the key tasks of the trainer is to help to develop these supportive features in the learning group.

## Diagnosis and setting individual goals

Chapter 5 describes three ways in which individual needs and goals for self-development may be identified. Other ways into this might include

—life planning (see chapter 3);

—examining particular difficulties that people have in their jobs;

—following on from activities such as 'Personal Journal' (Activity 6) and 'Analysis of Experiences' (Activity 12). Or, indeed, most of the book's activities can have a diagnostic function.

## Generating, identifying, and sharing resources

Clearly, the book's activities provide a number of resources to help meet the goals. However, in a group setting it is very helpful to get each individual to look on himself as a resource to others. By sharing experiences, giving data, listening, counselling, giving feedback, working as a pair-partner, members can be enormously helpful to one another. The trainer has an important role, not only in providing resources himself, but also in encouraging and helping everybody to help others. One simple way of initiating this is by writing individual goals on flip-chart paper, sticking these on the wall, and then getting each participant to write his name against those individual goals to which he feels he can make a contribution. As time goes on, members can be asked to examine the extent to which they have given help to, and received help from, others.

### Planning and meeting needs

On most conventional courses, the assumption is that everyone must go through a common programme. In so far as individual needs are considered at all, the approach is to establish a lowest common denominator so that everybody gets some needs met. The learning community, however, does not make this assumption, and tries to meet a wider range of individual needs by providing opportunities for different people to do different things—while at the same time maintaining a sense of group commitment and identity.

### Continuous evaluation

This is important on any course, but perhaps even more so when using a learning community approach. It is essential to get feedback and monitor progress in order to ensure that the supportive climate is being maintained and that individual goals are being met. Such evaluation must be relatively immediate and open—that is, the data are collected at frequent intervals (not only at the end of the event) and are immediately fed back to the group for discussion and action. (It's no use the trainer retreating to the safety of his room and furtively poring over the information, either ignoring its implications or, at best, determining to do 'something better next time'.)

Although a specific, discrete learning community can be very helpful for self-development, it still suffers from being a one-off, isolated event, separate from everyday work and life. This is a non-ideal state of affairs, since self-development, to be really successful, must be part of everything one does. We therefore prefer an approach that combines the elements of the learning community (i.e., supportive climate, diagnosis, resourcing, planning and action, continuous evaluation) with the participants' on-going work and life experiences. One way of doing this is by starting with a fairly short (e.g., one or two days) learning community event, after which participants use the activities and other resources in the context of their own jobs. Then, on a regular basis (say once a fortnight, or once a month), they meet again in a regular support group—on learning community lines—to help each other by sharing experiences, counselling, further diagnosis, feedback, and so on. Helping with these support groups provides a new and challenging role for the trainer—a role very similar to that described in connection with 'action learning', in Casey.[5]

## REFERENCES

1. Knowles, M. S., *The Adult Learner: A Neglected Species*, Gulf Publishing Co., 1973.
2. Boydell, T. H., *Experiential Learning* (Manchester Monograph No. 5). Dept. of Adult Education, University of Manchester, 1976.
3. Megginson, D. F. and M. J. Pedler, 'Developing structures and technology for the learning community', *Journal of European Training*, 5, 5, Winter, 1976.
4. Heron, J., *The Concept of a Peer Learning Community*, Human Potential Research Project, University of Surrey, 1974.
5. Casey, D., 'The emerging role of set adviser in action-learning programmes'. *Journal of European Training*, 5, 3, Summer, 1976.

*Printed in Great Britain at The Spottiswoode Ballantyne Press by William Clowes & Sons Limited London, Colchester and Beccles*